In
My Mother's
Kitchen

In My Mother's Kitchen

Writers on
Love, Cooking, and Family

Chamberlain Bros.
a member of Penguin Group (USA) Inc.
New York

CHAMBERLAIN BROS.
Published by the Penguin Group
Penguin Group (USA) Inc., 375 Hudson Street, New York, New York 10014, USA
Penguin Group (Canada), 90 Eglinton Avenue East, Suite 700, Toronto, Ontario
M4P 2Y3, Canada (a division of Pearson Penguin Canada Inc.)
Penguin Books Ltd, 80 Strand, London WC2R 0RL, England
Penguin Ireland, 25 St Stephen's Green, Dublin 2, Ireland
(a division of Penguin Books Ltd)
Penguin Group (Australia), 250 Camberwell Road, Camberwell, Victoria 3124,
Australia (a division of Pearson Australia Group Pty Ltd)
Penguin Books India Pvt Ltd, 11 Community Centre, Panchsheel Park,
New Delhi–110 017, India
Penguin Group (NZ), Cnr Airborne and Rosedale Roads, Albany, Auckland 1310,
New Zealand (a division of Pearson New Zealand Ltd)
Penguin Books (South Africa) (Pty) Ltd, 24 Sturdee Avenue, Rosebank,
Johannesburg 2196, South Africa

Penguin Books Ltd, Registered Offices: 80 Strand, London WC2R 0RL, England

Library of Congress Cataloging-in-Publication Data

In my mother's kitchen: writers on love, cooking, and family.
    p. cm.
   ISBN 1-59609-209-2
   1. Food.   2. Cookery.
TX355.5.I5   2006   2005051986
641.5—dc22

Printed in the United States of America
3 5 7 9 10 8 6 4 2

Book design by Jaime Putorti

Contents

CONTENTS

CONTENTS

In
My Mother's
Kitchen

The Measure of My Powers

M.F.K. Fisher

The first thing I cooked was pure poison. I made it for Mother, after my little brother David was born, and within twenty minutes of the first swallow, she was covered with great itching red welts. The doctor came, soda compresses were laid on, sedatives and mild physic were scattered about, and all subsided safely . . . except my feeling of deep shock and hurt professional pride. As the nurse, Miss Faulck, pointed out, I should have been content to let well enough alone.

The pudding was safe enough: a little round white shuddering milky thing I had made that morning under the stern eye of Miss Faulck and whoever it was that succeeded mad Ora in the kitchen. It had "set" correctly. It was made according to the directions for Invalid Cookery in Mother's best recipe book, and I had cleaned my fingernails until tears filled my eyes before I touched so much as a box of cornstarch.

Then, in the middle of the afternoon, when the pudding slid with a chill plop into the saucer, I knew that I could not stand to present it, my first culinary triumph, in its naked state. It was obscenely pure, obscenely colorless.

A kind of loyalty to Ora rose in me, and without telling Miss Faulck I ran into the backyard and picked ten soft ripe blackberries. I blew off the alley dust, and placed them gently in a perfect little circle around the little pudding. Its cool perfection leaped into sudden prettiness, like Miss America when the winning ribbon is hung across her high-breasted symmetry.

And even a little while later, when Mother lay covered with compresses and Miss Faulck pursed her lips and David howled for a meal he couldn't have because he might drink hive-juice, mother smiled at my shocked anxious confusion, and said, "Don't worry, sweet . . . it was the loveliest pudding I have ever seen."

I agreed with her in spite of the despair.

I can't remember ever learning anything, that is, I don't hear Mother's voice saying to me, "Now this is a teaspoon, and this is the way you sift flour, and warm eggs won't make mayonnaise. . . ." But evidently I loved to cook, and she taught me several things without making them into lessons, because in the next few years, I knew how to make white sauce, and cupcakes with grated orange rind in them. (Father was always very complimentary about them, and Anne and I loved to save ours until the rest of the family had left the table, and then cover them with cream and sugar and eat them with a spoon.)

I could even make jelly rolls, too, which seems odd now; I don't think I've ever tasted one since I was about ten, much less had any interest in putting one together.

I loved to read cookbooks (unlike my feeling for jelly roll, that passion has grown stronger with the years), and inevitably I soon started to improve on what I had read. Once I made poor Anne share my proud misery with something I called Hindu Eggs. I was sure I had read about it in Fanny Farmer; all you did was add curry powder to white sauce and pour it over sliced hardboiled eggs.

When Mother said that she and Father would be away one night, and I might get supper alone, I hid the gleam in my eye when she told me to put the sauce and the eggs in a casserole, and be sure to drink milk, and open a jar of plums or something for dessert.

"Yes, Mother, I know I can do it," I said smoothly, and the word "Hindu" danced sensuously in my mind, safely unsaid until Mother was out of the house.

The casserole was handsome, too, when Anne and I sat down to it in exciting solitude at the big table. Anne admired me, there was no doubt of it . . . and I admired myself. The rich brown sauce bubbled and sent out puffs of purely Oriental splendor. I sat in Father's place, and served each of us generously.

The first bite, and perhaps the next two or three, were all right; we were hungry, and in a hurry to feel the first warmth in our little bellies. Then Anne put down her fork. She beat me to it, so I continued to hold mine, determined like any honest cook to support my product.

"It's too hot, it burns," my little sister said, and gulped at her milk.

"Blow on it," I instructed. "Mother's not here."

We blew, and I ate three more bites to Anne's dutiful one. The heat seemed to increase. My influence over Anne must have been persuasive as well as autocratic in those far days, because she ate most of what was on her plate before the tears started rolling down her round brown cheeks.

I ate all mine, proudly; but inside I was cold with the new knowledge that I had been stupid. I had thought I remembered a recipe when I didn't, and I had used curry without knowing anything about it, and when the sauce looked boringly white I had proceeded to make it richly darker with probably five tablespoonfuls of the exotic powder.

I ate all I could, for fear Father would see how much we threw into the garbage pail, and then after my sweet forgiving little sister helped me straighten the kitchen we went upstairs and, with the desperate intuition of burned animals, sat on the edge of the bathtub with our mouths full of mineral oil. She never said anything more about it, either; and the next morning there were only a few blisters, just inside our lips.

When I was eleven we all moved to the country. We had a cow and chickens, and partly because of that and partly because Grandmother had died we began to eat more richly.

We had chocolate puddings with chopped nuts and heavy cream. The thought of them makes me dizzy now; but we loved them. And lots of butter: I was good at churning, and learned very well how to sterilize the wooden churn and make the butter and then roll it into fine balls and press it into molds. I liked that. And we could have mayonnaise, rich yellow with eggs and oil, instead of the boiled dressing Grandmother's despotic bowels and stern palate called for.

Mother, in an orgy of baking brought on probably by all the beautiful eggs and butter lying around, spent every Saturday morning making cakes. They were piled high with icings. They were filled with crushed almonds, chopped currants, and an outrageous number of calories. They were beautiful. Saturday afternoons they sat cooling, along with Mother and the kitchen after the hectic morning, and by Sunday night they were already a pleasant if somewhat bilious memory.

After about a year of this luscious routine, Mother retired more or less permanently to the front part of the house, perhaps with half an eye on the bathroom scales, but before she gave up cooking, I learned a lot about cakes from her. The fact that I have never made one since then—at least, the kind with many layers and fillings and icings and all that—has little to do with the gratitude I have often felt for knowing how to measure and sift and be patient and not be daunted by disappointment.

Mother, like all artists, was one-sided. She only cooked what she herself liked. She knew very little about meats, so I gradually learned that all by myself. She hated gravies, and any sauces but "white sauce" (probably a hangover from Grandmother's training), so I made some hideous mistakes with them. And there was always an element of surprise, if not actual danger, in my meals; the Hindu eggs had warned me but not curbed my helpless love of anything rare or racy.

But in spite of all that, I was the one who got dinner on the cook's off-night. I improved, there is no doubt about it, and it was taken for granted that I would step into the kitchen at the drop of a hat.

Perhaps Anne would have liked a chance at having all the family's attention for those few hours. If so she never got it. The stove, the bins, the cupboards, I had learned forever make an inviolable throne room. From them I ruled; temporarily I controlled. I felt powerful, and I loved that feeling.

I am more modest now, but I still think that one of the pleasantest of all emotions is to know that I, with my brain and my hands, have nourished my beloved few, that I have concocted a stew or a story, a rarity or a plain dish, to sustain them truly against the hungers of the world.

Bread-and-Butter Pudding

Nigel Slater

My mother is buttering bread for England. The vigor with which she slathers soft yellow fat onto thinly sliced white pap is as near as she gets to the pleasure that is cooking for someone you love. Right now she has the bread knife in her hand and nothing can stop her. She always buys unwrapped, unsliced bread, a pale sandwich loaf without much of a crust, and slices it by hand.

My mother's way of slicing and buttering has both an ease and an awkwardness about it. She has softened the butter on the back of the Aga range so that it forms a smooth wave as the butter knife is drawn across it. She spreads the butter onto the cut side of the loaf, then picks up the bread knife and takes off the buttered slice. She puts down the bread knife, picks up the butter knife, and again butters the freshly cut side of the loaf.

She carries on like this till she has used three-quarters of the loaf. The rest she will use in the morning, for toast.

The strange thing is that none of us really eats much bread and butter. It's like some ritual of good housekeeping that my mother has to go through. As if her grandmother's dying words had been "always make sure they have enough bread and butter on the table." No one ever sees what she does with all the slices we don't eat.

I mention all the leftover bread and butter to Mrs. Butler, a kind, gentle woman whose daughter is in my class at school and whose back garden has a pond with newts and goldfish, crowns of rhubarb, and rows of potatoes. A house that smells of apple crumble. I visit her daughter Madeleine at lunchtime and we often walk back to school together. Mrs. Butler lets me wait while Madeleine finishes her lunch.

"Well, your mum could make bread-and-butter pudding, apple charlotte, eggy bread, or bread pudding," suggests Mrs. Butler, "or she could turn them into toasted cheese sandwiches."

I love bread-and-butter pudding. I love its layers of sweet, quivering custard, juicy raisins, and puffed, golden crust. I love the way it sings quietly in the oven; the way it wobbles on the spoon.

You can't smell a hug. You can't hear a cuddle. But if you could, I reckon it would smell and sound of warm bread-and-butter pudding.

Maman's Cheese Soufflé

Jacques Pépin

When my mother got married, she was seventeen and my father was twenty-two. She did not know how to cook, except for a few simple dishes that she had learned from her mother. Yet she was willing and fearless.

My father liked cheese soufflé, so my mother graciously obliged. She had never made a soufflé before, but a friend told her that it consisted of a white sauce (béchamel), grated cheese, and eggs—a cinch! To the béchamel, that staple of the French home cook, she added her grated Swiss cheese and then cracked and added one egg after another to the mixture, stirred it well, poured it into a gratin dish, and baked it in the oven. *Voilà!* No one had told her that the eggs should be separated, with the yolks added to the base sauce and the whites whipped to a firm consistency and then gently folded into the mixture. Ignorance is bliss, and in this case it was indeed: the soufflé rose to a golden height and became a family favorite.

This is a great recipe; it can be assembled hours or even a day ahead, and although it is slightly less airy than a standard soufflé, it is delicious.

> 6 tablespoons (¾ stick) unsalted butter, plus
> more to butter a 6-cup gratin dish
> 6 tablespoons all-purpose flour
> 2 cups cold whole milk
> ½ teaspoon salt
> ½ teaspoon freshly ground black pepper
> 5 extra-large eggs
> 2½ cups grated Swiss cheese, preferably Gruyère
> (about 6 ounces)
> 3 tablespoons minced fresh chives

Preheat the oven to 400°F.

Butter a 6-cup gratin dish, and set it aside. Melt the butter in a saucepan, then add the flour, and mix it in well with a whisk. Cook for 10 seconds, add the milk in one stroke, and mix it in with a whisk. Keep stirring with the whisk until the mixture thickens and comes to a strong boil, which will take about 2 minutes. It should be thick and smooth. Remove from the heat, and stir in the salt and pepper. Allow about 10 minutes for the white sauce to cool.

Meanwhile, break the eggs into a bowl, and beat well with a fork. Add the eggs, the cheese, and the chives to the cooled sauce, and mix well to combine. Pour into the buttered gratin dish and cook immediately, or set aside until ready to cook.

Bake for 30 to 40 minutes, or until the soufflé is puffy and well browned on top. Although it will stay inflated for quite a while, it is best served immediately.

Serves 4.

The Assurance of Caramel Cake

Maya Angelou

Quilting bees were eagerly anticipated by Southern black women. They offered the only nonlabor, nonreligious occasions where women could gather and exchange all the communities' good and bad news. The women planned for weeks. Then they selected and cooked their favorite dessert dishes and brought them to the gathering. The bees were always held in the back of the store, which meant that Bailey and I could look forward to some delicious cakes and pies and, if the event took place in the summer, some luscious hand-cranked strawberry ice cream. Usually cranked by us.

Mrs. Sneed, the pastor's wife, would bring sweet potato pie, warm and a little too sweet for Momma's taste but perfect for Bailey and me. Mrs. Miller's coconut cake and Mrs. Kendrick's chocolate fudge were what Adam and Eve ate in the Garden just before the Fall. But the most divine dessert of all was Momma's Caramel Cake.

Momma would labor prayerfully over her selection, because she knew but would never admit that she and all the women were in hot competition over whose culinary masterpiece was the finest.

Momma could bake all the other women's dishes and often made them for the family, but not one of the other cooks would even dare the Caramel Cake (always to be spoken of in capital letters). Since she didn't have brown sugar, she had to make her own caramel syrup. Making her caramel cake took four to five hours, but the result was worthy of the labor. The salty sweetness of the caramel frosting along with the richness of the batter made the dessert soften and liquefy on the tongue and slip quietly down the throat almost without notice. Save that it left a memory of heaven itself in the mouth.

Of course Bailey and I were a little biased in Momma's favor, but who could have resisted the bighearted woman who was taller and bigger than most men yet who spoke in a voice a little above a whisper? Her hands were so large one could span my entire head, but they were so gentle that when she rubbed my legs and arms and face with blue-seal Vaseline every morning, I felt as if an angel had just approved of me.

I not only loved her, I liked her. So I followed her around. People began calling me her shadow.

"Hello, Sister Henderson, I see you got your shadow with you as usual." She would smile and answer, "I guess you got that right. If I go, she goes. If I stop, she stops. Yes, sir, I have me two shadows. Well, three by rights. My own and my two grandbabies."

I only saw Momma's anger become physical once. The incident alarmed me, but at the same time it assured me that I had great protection. Because of a horrible sexual violence I experienced when I was seven, I stopped talking to everyone but Bailey.

All teachers who came to Stamps to work at Lafayette County Training School had to find room and board with black families, for there were no boardinghouses where they could gain admittance.

All renting families acted as individual chambers of commerce for the newcomers. Each teacher was told of the churches and the preachers, of the hairdressers and barbers, of the white store downtown and the Wm. Johnson General Merchandise Store where they were likely to get accounts to tide them over between paychecks. The new teachers were also alerted to Mrs. Henderson's mute granddaughter and her grandson who stuttered seriously.

Summer was over and we returned to school with all the other children. I looked forward to meeting the new teacher of the fourth-, fifth-, and sixth-grade classes. I was really happy because for the first time Bailey and I were in the same classroom.

Miss Williams was small and perky. She reminded me of a young chicken pecking in the yard. Her voice was high-pitched. She separated the classes by row. Sixth-graders sat near the windows, fifth-graders were in the middle rows, and fourth-graders were near the door.

Miss Williams said she wanted each student to stand up and say his or her name and what grades they received at the end of the last semester.

She started with the sixth-graders. I looked at Bailey when he stood and said, "Bailey Johnson, Jr." At home he would make me fall out laughing when he said what he wished his whole name was: "Bailey James Jester Jonathan Johnson, Jr."

Because I didn't talk I had developed a pattern of behavior in classrooms. Whenever I was questioned, I wrote my answer on the blackboard. I had reached the blackboard in Miss Williams's room when the teacher approached me. We were nearly the same height.

She said, "Go back to your seat. Go on."

Bailey stood up over by the windows.

He said, "She's going to write her name and grade on the blackboard."

Miss Williams said to me, "I've heard about you. You can talk, but you just *won't* talk."

The students, who usually teased me relentlessly, were on my side. They began explaining, "She never talks, Miss Williams, never." Bailey was nervous. He began to stutter, "My . . . Maya can't talk."

Miss Williams said, "You will talk in my classroom. Yes, you will." I didn't know what to do. Bailey and the other children were trying to persuade her to allow me to write on the blackboard. I did not resist as she took the chalk out of my hand. "I know you can talk. And I will not stand for your silliness in my classroom." I watched her as she made herself angry. "You will not be treated differently just because your people own a store."

"Speak, speak." She was fairly shouting. Her hand came up unexpectedly and she slapped me. Truly, I had not known what to do when she was winding herself up to hit me, but I knew what I had to do the second her hand landed on my cheek. I ran. I ran out of the classroom with Bailey following, shouting, "Wait, My, wait." I couldn't wait. I was running to Momma. He caught up with me on the porch of the store.

Momma, hearing the noise, opened the screen door.

"What happened? Why aren't you in school? Sister, why are you crying?"

Bailey tried to answer her, but his brain moved faster than his tongue could form the words.

I took my notebook and pencil and wrote, "Miss Williams slapped me because I wouldn't talk."

"She slapped you? Slapped? Where?"

Bailey said, "FA . . . fa . . . fa . . . face."

Momma told Bailey to go back to school. She said she and I would be coming soon.

Momma's calm voice and unhurried manner helped Bailey to settle down enough to speak.

"You want me to tell Miss Williams that you are coming?"

Momma answered, "I want you to go back to school and get your lessons." He looked at me once, saw that I had stopped crying, so he nodded and jumped off the porch and headed back up the hill.

"Sister, go to the well and put some fresh water on your face." I went around behind the store to the well.

When I returned to the porch Momma had put on one of her huge freshly washed, starched, sun-dried, and ironed aprons. In her hand she had the board that was slipped into pockets closing off the front door. We had a similar plank for the store, which we used every night to let customers know we were closed. I don't remember there being a lock for the house or the store.

Momma dropped the board into the slots, and in a second she was striding up the hill to the school.

I hurried beside, hoping to read her intentions on her face.

She looked as she always looked, serene, quiet. If she planned something unusual it did not register on her face.

She walked into the school building and turned around to me.

"Sister, show me your classroom."

I guided her to Miss Williams's room. She opened the door and Miss Williams walked up to Momma.

She asked, "Yes? May I help you?"

My grandmother asked, "Are you Miss Williams?"

Miss Williams said, "I am."

Momma asked, "Are you somebody's grandbaby?"

Miss Williams answered, "I am someone's granddaughter."

Momma said, "Well, this child here is my grandbaby." Then she slapped her. Not full force, but hard enough for the sound to go around the room and to elicit gasps from the students.

"Now, Sister, nobody has the right to hit nobody in the face. So I am wrong this time, but I'm teaching a lesson." She looked at me. "Now find yourself a seat and sit down and get your lesson."

Momma left the room and it was suddenly empty and very quiet.

Miss Williams left the room for a few minutes. Not a word was spoken.

Miss Williams reentered and said, "Students, turn to lesson one on page one."

I looked at Bailey and he gave me the smallest nod. I turned to page one, lesson one.

No one spoke of the incident on the way home, and when I returned to the store, Momma and Uncle Willie were sitting on the porch.

Uncle Willie said, "Sister, there's something on the kitchen table. Bring it out here please."

I went into the kitchen and on the chopping table stood the most wondrous Caramel Cake looking like paradise, oozing sweetness.

Carefully I brought it back to the porch and it was nearly worth being slapped just to hear Bailey gasp.

Uncle Willie said, "This cake can't pay you for being slapped in the face. Momma made it just to tell you how much we love you and how precious you are."

CARAMEL CAKE

8 tablespoons (1 stick) butter

1 1/4 cups sugar

1/4 cup Caramel syrup (recipe follows)

2 cups sifted all-purpose flour

2 teaspoons baking powder

½ teaspoon salt

1 cup milk

2 large eggs

Caramel frosting (recipe follows)

Preheat oven to 375°F. Line two 8-inch layer cake pans with greased wax paper.

In large mixing bowl, beat butter, and add 1 cup sugar gradually until light and fluffy. Beat in syrup.

In medium mixing bowl, sift flour, baking powder, and salt together. Add sifted ingredients to creamed mixture, alternating with milk.

In separate medium mixing bowl, beat eggs about 3 minutes, until foamy. Add remaining sugar, and beat until there is a fine spongy foam. Stir into cake batter until blended.

Divide batter between cake pans. Bake for about 25 minutes. Remove pans from oven. Gently press center of cake with forefinger. Cake should spring back when finger is removed. If it doesn't, return to oven for 10 minutes. Cool in pans for 10 minutes. Turn out onto rack, and remove wax paper. Let cakes cool to room temperature before frosting.

To assemble: Center one cooled cake layer on cake plate. Cover top and sides with generous helpings of frosting. Place second layer evenly on frosted layer. Repeat frosting procedure. Make certain that sides are completely frosted. Cool in refrigerator until ready to serve.

Serves 8.

CARAMEL SYRUP

1 cup white sugar

1 cup boiling water

Heat sugar in heavy skillet over low heat. Stir constantly until melted to a brown liquid. When it bubbles over entire surface, remove from heat. Slowly add boiling water, stirring constantly. Pour into container and cool.

CARAMEL FROSTING

6 tablespoons (¾ stick) butter

One 8-ounce package confectioners' sugar

4 tablespoons heavy cream

1½ teaspoons vanilla extract

Pinch of salt

Brown butter in heavy pot over medium heat—be vigilant or it will burn. Allow butter to cool. In large mixing bowl, add confectioners' sugar, cream, vanilla extract, and salt to the butter, and beat until smooth. If frosting is too stiff, add tablespoon of half-and-half or full cream to thin.

The Queen of Sheba

Jennifer Appel

For those of you unfamiliar with the decadent Queen of Sheba cake (*Reine de Saba*), let me introduce you. An overwhelmingly delectable French torte, simultaneously wicked and divine. Perhaps I'm overstating, but I don't really think so. After a decade in the food business and dozens of turns baking this cake, I still don't think I come close to my mother's version of this confection.

My mother is an expert cook. I was raised in a time when many mothers were housewives and still cooked dinner every night. My mother cooked every night, and I don't think she ever repeated a dinner recipe in any given month. She constantly had ideas up her sleeve. I recall other friends' houses always smelling of furniture polish or cigarette smoke, but ours always smelled of food. We used to say, "If there was an onion in the house, there was a meal." And with my mother, that meal was sure to be sophisticated, creative, and above all, delicious. We never knew how good we had it.

My mother's cooking skills were at her finest when it came to the food she made for my sister Sharon's engagement party. The date was May 22, 1977. I know this because my mother knows this; she is of the uncanny ability to recall all significant dates and all relatively insignificant details. While the idea had floated around for a while that we should have my sister's engagement party professionally catered, my father simply asked Mom if she would do it instead. She replied, "Okay!" In an almost Herculean display of will and strength she had poured every ounce of herself into preparing for that day. Only a week prior, her mother, my grandmother, had undergone surgery, so for my sister's sake, and the sake of the guests, my mother had to keep her mind off her very real troubles. But she held nothing back to make this day as perfect as it could possibly be.

There was an absolutely beautiful table, decorated with a magnificent basket of white flowers and fine china. Even the napkins were colorful and pretty. There was a large punch bowl, champagne, piña coladas, wines, and soft drinks. People had come from all over to offer my sister and her fiancé, Mark, their congratulations and best wishes, showering them with gifts. (In case you may be wondering, they celebrated twenty-seven years in June 2005.) Amid all the relative chaos of having almost one hundred people in our home, my mother had made every single possible dish that was placed on the table for our guests.

Everything.

"I don't know where I took the energy from, but I got it all done," she recalls. And with a usual dig at her rather bookish daughter, she says, "I don't think you helped with *anything.*"

Sadly, this could very well be true. I often believe whatever culinary talents I seem to possess I must have gleaned through osmosis from the hours upon hours of just simply watching my mother work.

She made potato salad, vegetable salad, green salad, Russian salad with red beets. Even her vinaigrette dressing was made from scratch (a recipe which I continue to make to this day). There were the onion quiches, broccoli quiches, pigs in blankets, sliced turkey, roast beef, corned beef with freshly baked rolls. The sheer quantity of food was stupendous, and we even rented an extra refrigerator and kept it in the garage! At least my mother wasn't foolish enough to think she could serve all this herself; we did have some hired help for service and washing.

But if that wasn't enough, she made, from scratch, about fifteen desserts. There was her especially renowned pound cake, *palatschinken*, a Swiss broyage, a genoise, a Jell-O mold with celery and cranberries, *kirschenmichel*, a cheesecake, fresh whipped cream, fruit salad, and an incredible assortment of mouthwatering tortes.

And, sprung from the pages of the legendary Julia Child's *Mastering the Art of French Cooking, Vol. 1* . . . the Queen of Sheba.

Now, before we continue, it ought to be noted the Queen of Sheba cake is not for the faint of heart or clogged of artery. In fact, I'm fairly certain, if need be, the Queen of Sheba cake could potentially be used as an effective lethal weapon. With its thick, moist fudge center just slightly underbaked, smothered in thick, delicious chocolate butter cream, with blanched almonds pressed comfortably into its edges, a Surgeon General's warning could certainly be warranted. I believe the nutritional information looks something like this:

NUTRITIONAL INFORMATION

Calories: A billion!

Total Fat: 720 g

Saturated Fat: 700 g

Cholesterol: Avert your eyes!

Carbohydrates: You *don't* want to know.

Oh, but to a precocious twelve-year-old girl these things are of no consequence. The temptation was too strong: A slice of this cake had to be stuffed into my mouth, and, I should add, immediately.

With what seemed like an endless stream of people flooding into the house, pouring over into our backyard, my cousin Ellen (the only other person there my age) and I began our reconnaissance mission. We waited patiently for the moment when my mother would exit the kitchen to attend to the party's guests. When our opportunity finally came, we quietly crept across the kitchen toward the refrigerator, completely unnoticed by anyone.

When we reached the refrigerator, I prepared to show Ellen all the food, probably to boast how my mother had made this stupendous array all by herself. I slowly and quietly opened the refrigerator door . . . *and there it was!* A freshly baked Queen of Sheba cake cooling in all its sinful glory beneath a thin sheet of aluminum foil. "That dessert," I said, "is my favorite dessert. Let's have a piece now."

I gently lifted the delicate tinfoil, then slowly made my way to swipe a kitchen knife, and cut myself (and Ellen, I suppose) a small sliver of the Queen of Sheba cake. Ellen and I, two mischievous twelve-year-olds without the necessary conscience to stop us, then proceeded to run off, so we could devour this treasure of a slice before lunch was even served. In my mind, it was the most sinfully decadent, thickly fudgy chocolate cake you could ever imagine.

As usual, we didn't know how good we had it. My mother being the master baker she is knows exactly how to make this cake and we were wide-eyed with delight. "Wow," said Ellen, "that's the best chocolate cake I ever tasted."

Prep time: 35 minutes

Cook time: 25 minutes

Eating time: Approximately 15 seconds

A few moments later, I heard my mother calling loudly from the kitchen: "Who ate a slice of the cake!? What happened to my cake!"

Thankfully, she was too busy to look for the culprits.

But aside from the delicious taste of that slice of Queen of Sheba that day, I can distinctly remember being in absolute awe of my mother. That she could have cooked and baked and served so many delicious dishes and desserts and entertained for so many people is beyond my comprehension. And though this may come as some surprise to my mother, who believes I never saw a darned thing going on in that kitchen, it was my mother with all her infinite talents who inspired me to open my bakeries and it is she to whom I owe it all.

Martha Washington's Great Cake

Mount Vernon Estate and Gardens

The Great Cake was a Washington family favorite, and was served during the Christmas holidays and for other special occasions. This recipe has been adapted for the twenty-first century.

> 10 eggs
>
> 1 lb. butter
>
> 1 lb. sugar
>
> 1 1/4 lbs. flour
>
> 1 1/4 lbs. chopped fruit & nuts
>
> 2 1/2 tsp. ground mace
>
> 2 1/2 tsp. ground nutmeg
>
> 2 oz. wine
>
> 2 oz. French brandy

Preheat oven to 350°F. Separate eggs and set yolks aside. Beat egg whites to form a soft peak. Cream the butter. Slowly add the beaten egg whites, one spoonful at a time, to the butter. Slowly add the sugar to the butter and egg white mixture, one spoonful at a time. Add egg yolks. Slowly fold in flour. Stir in fresh or dried fruit and nuts, then mace, nutmeg, wine, and brandy. Bake in a greased and floured 10" springform cake pan for about 75 minutes. Allow cake to cool, and remove it from the pan.

ICING

Beat 3 egg whites and 2 Tbsp. powdered sugar until egg whites are stiff but not dry. Continue to beat in sugar until you have added 1½ cups. Add 1 tsp. grated lemon peel and 2 Tbsp. orange flower water. Beat until the icing is stiff enough to stay parted when a knife cuts through it. Smooth it onto the cake. Let it dry and harden in a 200°F oven for 1 hour. Icing will be brittle (like a meringue) when cut with a knife.

In My Mother's Kitchen: Reminiscences

Walter Staib

It was in my mother's kitchen that I discovered as a very young child what would be my lifelong passion, food and drink, and her influence and guidance there set me off on my career as a professional chef. As most people do, especially young children, I learned my craft from the mistakes I made working together with my mother in the kitchen. The lessons I learned from the many experiences we shared together gave me a great start in life and were very valuable, not just in my profession, but in life.

I grew up in Pforzheim, Germany, which is right on the border with France and is the gateway to the fabled Black Forest region. We lived with my mother's family, the Breuningers, in a large house with many members of our extended family— aunts, uncles, cousins—all under one roof. I was born right after World War II, so, obviously, while I was growing up everything was scarce, especially food, but we were more fortunate than most because my grandfather, whose roots traced back to Burgundy, was a bon vivant who appreciated fine food and drink. Even though times were tough, my grandfather believed in multicourse meals with the full complement of beverages—aperitif, wine with dinner, and a digestif afterward. (When I was young, I always believed that when you got older a beret would grow out of your head because I never saw him without one, except at the dinner table.)

So, we had livestock (goats, sheep, pigs, chickens), orchards, and vegetable gardens, some right next to our house and some in remote locations around town, which is the norm in many European cities. We believed in eating "from the farm to the table," which was the only way we knew to make food, and, in the postwar environment, the only way to survive, really. We even made our own eau-de-vie, hard cider, and table wine.

Everything we did was rooted in tradition and dictated by age-old rituals. No one talked during dinner, everyone had his own seat, and my grandfather, as the patriarch, carved the meat and portioned out the food according to age and rank.

Having grown up in this environment, my mother excelled in the kitchen at a young age, learning how to cook from my grandmother, using my great-grandmother's recipes. She learned by helping her mother, which is how I was to learn. My only uncle, Walter, was killed in World War II, leaving me the only other male in the family aside from my grandfather. That meant that I began helping out at a much younger age than usual. At the tender age of four, I ended up doing many chores that somehow always ended up in the kitchen.

Thanks to this early exposure, there was never any doubt in my mind that my quest in life was to become a chef and excel as a chef. My devotion to culinary arts was reinforced when my aunt Ruth married into a family who owned a successful restaurant, Gasthaus von Buckenburg, which also had its own gigantic butcher shop. I spent a lot of time there with my grandfather, observing a different type of cooking, which was even more intriguing than the home kitchen.

Since the Breuninger family was well known for their culinary prowess, my grandmother and mother were asked many times to go to cook for other people in their homes for weddings, confirmations, and other large important gatherings. As you can imagine, I often went along to assist with odd jobs, such as peeling carrots and garlic, and other small duties that a four- or five-year-old could easily master.

When I was about five years old, my mother was asked to

cook at a home in a village nearly forty minutes away from our hometown. It was for a confirmation party and she was responsible for providing a feast for thirty to forty people. The menu, as always, was prearranged to be sure that all the ingredients my mother needed would be there before she arrived. As in most cases, this was a menu of typical Black Forest fare.

We took the bus there and by the time we arrived my mother was pretty stressed out, and I'm sure I didn't help by asking millions of questions while she was trying to get set up. The first course for the dinner was *flädlessupp*, a homemade chicken consommé, with *crèpes aux fines herbes* sliced up and placed in the soup just before serving. She set to boil a large pot of chicken gizzards with carrots, onion, and celery root, and gave me the job of straining vegetables and gizzards out of the soup when it had the right flavor.

She also instructed me to pick the gizzards out of the vegetables and save the gizzards on the side. Being five years old and not understanding why I needed to follow this particular direction, I decided that they were too hot to pick out and I dumped the vegetables and gizzards into the trash can. When my mother came back to the kitchen, she told me, "Let me know when they cool enough and I'll show you how to cut them." This put me in a quick frenzy and I dug furiously through the garbage can to find all of the gizzards. Though I'm sure I didn't find them all, I did find most of them, washed them off in the sink, and pretended that nothing had ever happened.

Needless to say, the soup was saved, served, and a complete success, as was the rest of the dinner.

I always thought I fooled her, but much later she told me that she knew what was happening and congratulated me on not breaking down like a normal five-year-old might, but showing some ingenuity and doing what had to be done. I didn't get punished, but I didn't need to. It taught me an important lesson early on to listen and follow directions from someone with experience, even if it didn't seem to make sense to do so. This served me well in later years when I was doing my culinary apprenticeships and gave me a significant edge over my fellow apprentices.

Another time, we were at home at my grandparents' house. (Remember, we all lived together in a big house, so celebrations of holidays, religious events, and rites of passage almost always took place at our house.) This particular event was an engagement party for one of my aunts. My mother and grandmother spent hours planning the menu and were in charge of all the food for the great feast, while my grandfather carefully chose all the proper wines and spirits for each course, no doubt with quite a bit of hands-on research! It was, as usual, to be a smorgasbord worthy of any grand five-star hotel, and the pièce de résistance was a large stuffed veal breast that my grandfather would carve at the table with great ceremony.

Stuffed veal breast is not an easy thing to make. It takes hours of chopping and slicing, making the stuffing, stuffing the breast, sewing up any holes in the breast, and then hours roasting in the oven. It's also not cheap, so every attempt at making a veal breast, especially during a time of scarcity and frugality, just has to turn out perfectly.

That morning, my grandmother went to my uncle's butcher shop to hand select the veal breast she wanted to use. Meanwhile, my mother was in the kitchen preparing the stuffing—chopping up onions, carrots, celery root, and so on—which had to be cooked, cooled, and stuffed into the breast. Then, any punctures made in the breast had to be sewn up so the stuffing wouldn't come out.

Once the breast was stuffed and it was time for my mother to begin preparing other things, she gave me the important task of keeping an eye on the veal breast while it was roasting in the oven. We had a coal-fired oven, so we really had to pay close attention to anything that we were baking or roasting to make sure it didn't burn or overcook. All I had to do was baste the veal breast frequently and make sure it didn't burn.

While my mother and grandmother were running around doing other things in the other room, I was left pretty much on my own. As any child of a very smart parent can attest, my mother had made watching the veal breast seem like an exciting task, like Huck Finn whitewashing the fence. It was fun at first, but eventually I got bored just sitting there, pouring the drippings over the veal breast every ten minutes or so. In my mind, I was begging for some attractive diversion.

Soon enough, and much to my delight, one of my friends called to me from the courtyard behind our house, soccer ball in hand and ready to kick the ball around. Using my five-year-old logic, I figured it wouldn't hurt to go kick the ball around between bastings. When you're five or six years old, the concept of time management doesn't exist and the time passed more quickly than I realized. When I came back to baste the veal breast it was completely scorched—black as the coal that fired the oven. There was no covering up this mistake because it wasn't a question of just picking something out of the trash. A feeling of dread washed over me.

My grandmother came back into the room and quickly discovered what I had done, or rather not done. I tried to blame my friend for seducing me away from my work, hoping that such a weak excuse would save me, but it didn't fly. She sounded the alarm and I ended up with a spanking from grandfather, which seemed a bit extreme to me at the time.

The dinner was still a success even though the veal breast was kind of dry on top and I was a pariah for the rest of the day. The experience taught me a valuable lesson, though. When you put so much work into something, you have to follow through, no matter how difficult or boring it may seem at the end. What's more, you have to take every task seriously, no matter how small because, as they say, "God (and the Devil, too) is in the details."

Growing up part of a large extended family (my mother had eight siblings whose families—husbands, wives, and children—all lived with us), the Sunday meal was a big event, an occasion that was taken very seriously because friends of the family often joined us. The menu was always planned out at least by Wednesday and depended on the season, since we raised or grew practically everything we ate.

One Sunday sticks out in my mind more than others. It was November or December and freezing cold out, so we were going to enjoy a rather hearty meal—beef rouladen, brussels sprouts, which we call *rosenkohl*, or rose cabbage, and bread dumplings. Since my grandfather was the custodian of our church, we spent longer at church than anyone else, so the meal had to be practically prepared before we left for church, leaving just a small amount of finishing before dinner when we returned.

I was always eager to help my mother, especially to roll up the beef rouladen, which was fun for a youngster. It was even more fun when she let me brown them off in the pan because that was real cooking, so I was looking forward to my task. My mother, however, had something else in mind for me that Sunday—the brussels sprouts.

In those days, we grew brussels sprouts in our garden because they were a great low-maintenance winter vegetable. You just left them in the field and picked the frozen sprouts off the stalks as needed. The only problem was that it had to be done with bare hands because mittens or gloves made it impossible to get a good grip on the sprouts. Well, much to my disappointment, that was the task my mother assigned me.

She gave me a large bowl and sent me out to the garden to fill up the bowl with brussels sprouts. I put on my coat and went outside into the bone-chilling wind and tromped through the snow to the garden. Teeth chattering from the cold, I had an epiphany and snuck back into the kitchen and got a smaller bowl, which I dutifully filled to the brim with the sprouts. I put the bowl on the counter and ran upstairs to join the rest of my family in getting ready for church.

When she asked me later on if I picked the brussels sprouts, I said, "Yes, they're in the kitchen." When we got back from church my mother went immediately to the kitchen to finish dinner, and immediately discovered that I had switched the bowls on her. It was too late to pick more because there wasn't enough time for them to defrost, so everyone got only a paltry two or three on their plate. The good news was that my mother didn't "rat me out" or shame me in front of the guests, as most parents at least threaten to do. Instead, I lost my twenty cents allowance for a couple of weeks.

I learned right then and there that I shouldn't take the easy way out.

My last remembrance is of a time when my aunt Christa, who is only seven years older than me and was more like a sister to me, and I were home alone. We were bored, and since we had always watched my mother and grandmother make bonbons with caramel, we decided to take a stab at it. We knew where the sugar jar was kept, so that was easy. The challenge, then, was to get some milk.

The only way to get milk was to go out to the stable and milk the goat, which was my first attempt ever at milking a goat. Needless to say, I didn't get a drop of milk out of the goat, but did get a few nice bruises from being kicked. Not about to be deterred by an uncooperative goat, we marched next door and borrowed a quart of milk from the neighbors.

With all the ingredients at hand, and thinking that this was going to be a piece of cake, we started to cook the sugar and milk. What we didn't realize was how fast the caramel turns from gold to black, to flames! Luckily, my aunt had the presence of mind to put a cover over the pot to put out the flames. We were lucky that we didn't burn down the entire kitchen.

We ran around frantically opening windows and fanning the air with towels, but the entire house smelled like burnt sugar. The odor wouldn't dissipate no matter what we did, so there was a lot of explaining to do once the adults came back, because not only did we almost burn down the house, we wasted valuable milk and sugar. Our punishment was to be banned from the kitchen for quite some time, and we got strict orders never to cook by ourselves again, but my mother did tell me that the next time she made caramel bonbons she would let us help so that we could learn how to do them without endangering our lives!

This experiment taught us both that when you see something on the surface, it's not often as simple as it seems. Later on, I appreciated taking my time to really understand thoroughly how something is done. I discovered that asking questions is essential—the more you ask, the more you learn.

I'm glad I had the chance to spend so much time in the kitchen with my mother because it taught me life's lessons at an early age, which ensured my success at every stage in my development. When she visits me this year, I look forward to cooking with her in *my* kitchen!

South Indian Filter Coffee with Amma

Julie Sahni

As far back as I can remember, I have loved milk, not because our Indian Vedic ancestors four thousand years ago preached its virtues as God's favorite food and declared it an elixir "amtrita," but because my childhood and much of my younger years were wrapped in sweet and sensuous experiences surrounding milk, which linger in my memory and remain as fresh today as the first ray of sunrise on Ganjus.

I like milk in all forms: in creamy pudding *kheer*, refreshing frozen ice milk *kulfi*, thick fudge-cake *barfi*, caramelized sauce *rabri*, and milk-punch *Thandai*. I love to sip warm and frothy milk with a hint of Indian natural sugar, jaggery *gur*, a little crushed Malabar green cardamom, and a tiny pinch of Kashmir saffron. And when I am emotionally drained to my roots, I reach for a pot, pour some milk in, and place it on the stove. Just a whiff of that delicate fragrance rising above the simmering milk magically transports me into a cosmic world, soothing and comforting my aching soul. There are times when I let the milk boil down, to evaporate its moisture and turn into a caramelized fudge, thick with that hypnotic *khoya* aroma, which I devour with slices of tart Granny Smith apples. Other times I add an itsy bit of a dark, opaque decoction and turn it into a milky South Indian filter coffee. The roasted Mysore coffee beans from my mother's kitchen and her three-quarters-century-old brewing technique are essential ingredients of this recipe, straight from heaven!

My mother, Amma, is a foodie. She isn't just fond of it, but obsessed with it. Lucky me that of all her daughters, my mother believes, I ended up with that special gene. You can imagine the food adventures that awaited a child so blessed!

Most flights from New York to New Delhi arrive late in the evening, and by the time one clears customs and immigration, gets out of the airport, and starts the long drive home, it is way past bedtime. Maybe it is the Delhi air, or the jet lag, or simply that I am not an early riser, but leaving the cozy comforter at the crack of dawn, in the January chill, is not an easy task, even as my ears and brains get pounded with jarring bells and *bhajans* (devotional songs) from the local temple and the loud *maulvi's azan* from the neighborhood mosque, announcing, "Wake up!" To add to this musical chorus are a yoga instructor's chants from the neighboring house's TV. Piercing voices coming right at me, coaxing me to breathe deep, stretch, and form an *asanana* (in my language it means twist into a pretzel!). I am more exhausted. Instantly I pull the cover over, curl up like a snail, my favorite position, and slip back into my blissful dream world.

"Julu, come smell the coffee," my mother whispers in my ear; I lay there tired as a deadmeat, but contemplating, only for a brief moment though. There is no way I was going to miss the pleasure of my mother's coffee, not today, not any day, never.

My mother, an early riser, is already busy setting up the coffee filter, picking lentils clean of stones. Finding that little bugger is a task no one wants because they look almost identical in color and shape to lentils. Not an accident of nature but a deliberate attempt of some crafty suppliers to weigh-up lentils, thus increasing their profit margin. Not a single stone ever escapes my mother's twenty-twenty vision. Yes, it is her natural eyesight, free of spectacles, contact lenses, or surgery. The lentils are washed and added to a deep pot along with plenty of water to ensure slow, uncovered cooking. In January fresh turmeric rhizome is in season, and she adds a few slices—

otherwise it's just dry powder and a spoonful of her favorite virgin sesame oil from the neighborhood oil press *kolhu*. The cooked lentils will later get combined with spices, tamarind, tiny eggplants, and shallots to be transformed into the spicy stew *sambaar* that is a quintessential accompaniment to the mild and airy rice-and-bean dumplings *idlee*. My mother often whips up cilantro chutney with the garlicky spice *asafetida* that is to die for.

The coffee decoction is almost ready and I am getting hungrier by the minute. My mother and I wait patiently for the milkman to ring the doorbell. For one brief moment I leave the present, the kitchen, the cooking lentils, and travel back in time, taking my mother by my side.

It is a cool winter morning in Kanpur, a small town on the bank of Ganjus. I am standing by my mother's side, reaching barely to her waist, waiting for the milkman to arrive. It is a time when things get done at a difference pace, and in different ways. You want milk; you bring the cow, literally. Our cow, *Chandarmukhi*, meaning "beautiful as a moon," is tended by the cowherd, or the milkman, Lallan. She supplies the milk for our family every day, twice a day. My mother's kitchen is semi-rural and has enough area and facilities around it for the cow. She is painted pretty in vivid colors and adorned with bells that jingle with her every movement. Often her adorable calf accompanies her because that allows milk to flow more readily, thus making Lallan's job easier. Lallan strokes his cow tenderly, whispering flattering words, coaxing her to part with her milk. "Oh, my moon-face, why are you acting mean, like wretched in-laws? You are my sweet and beautiful—I save the best massages and fodder for you." It is like a secret pact between them; soon thereafter, even without the presence of the calf, the milk flows down her udders, which Lallan, sitting on his tippy toes, collects in a bucket.

My mother makes sure I get a handful, straight from the cow. The taste of the raw milk, still warm and frothy, is embedded in my mind.

One time Lallan could not come to us, so my mother and I paid a visit to his barn. Lined with shady *jamun* (an Indian purple-colored fruit) trees, the barn smelled sweet of hay, earth, and fresh milk. Under a tree stood *Chandarmukhi* with her playful calf, but she was done for the day giving milk. Just then Lallan informed us that we were to get buffalo's milk. As a child I used to love stroking the cow, but I was warned to be careful with buffalo. Moody and ill-tempered, they were difficult to milk. I didn't count, but that day Lallan got kicked by the buffalo with his hind legs enough times that he needed treatment for minor cuts. But we did get the milk and made it back home. The taste of that milk, a scent so pure and primal, is what I yearn for every day.

Two liters of milk in plastic pouches is just enough to take care of the need for breakfast and lunch. The milkman hands over the ice-cold milk pouches to my mother. He will repeat the same process later that afternoon, bringing another set quantity that will be used for evening tea and dinner, for entertaining and emergencies. Crisis arises when milk is not used up to the last drop, every day. An Indian cannot bring him- or herself to discard milk. Period. My mother brings out her milk-donor/receiver list. At the top is my sister. Ignoring all protests that her kitchen is already overflowing, the milk is readied, packed, and sent off. My sister will turn it into a pudding or a sweet for dinner.

I have wondered in the past why my mother would not pick up the milk herself from the MotherDairy store just a few blocks away and store it in her fabulous refrigerator that lies practically empty. There are also electrical appliances and gadgets to "zip through" cooking. In addition to the milkman, she has a person to wash dishes, sweep the floor, clean house, do laundry, iron clothes, and tend to her garden that is blooming with jasmine, Indian champa, lilies, rose, dahlia, and several varieties of kari plants. I have volunteered to do dishes, vacuum, and sweep the floor, dust furniture, and wipe the Delhi soot off the windows.

When questioned, my mother's answers are well thought out and reasoned. "Sure, I can fetch the milk myself," she explains, "but by giving this chore to this young man, I have added him to the workforce." She points out that the entire neighborhood is doing the same and that he is "earning the money," and not getting a handout. "Employing a person is the best thing one can do for this country and for its people. This is how we are going to build self-worth and esteem," my mother says, pointing to the fact that this milkman can now support his family, send kids to school who can aspire, not just dream, to achieve anything they want. About the second part of the question, she is more philosophical. "There is something very tangible I see in lentils," she continues. "When they are boiled, slowly, in the correct pan and at the proper temperature, they cook gradually, from hard, to semihard, to medium-soft, to very soft. You need to watch them when they are cooking, adding water if they begin to look dry. Maintaining correct liquid levels is necessary to produce creamy and plump lentils." She is so correct; it takes real attention and patience to master that technique. Yes, it is only a bowl of cooked lentils, but they are perfectly cooked, and when you take a spoonful in your mouth and let it glide and slosh, the savory sensation is reminiscent of butter-poached oysters!

"Do you know the food we cook evolves and transforms, gracefully, in stages, just as we all do?" my mother points out. "You pay attention to detail and you have a recipe for success, both in food and life. This is the reality I see each time I cook my ordinary way." By "ordinary" she means traditional, and what an extraordinary way that is.

I love to watch my mother cook: in my professional kitchen in New York; in my sister's kitchen, fitted with state-of-the-art gadgetry for slow, speedy, and pressure cooking; or, best of all, in her own in New Delhi, lined with jars of spices, grains, and legumes and neat rows of stainless-steel, brass, aluminum, and iron cookware, all traditional style, all made in India, all with glowing patina.

Fully attired in a lovely Kanjivaram sari in peacock blue silk with a mustard-colored temple border, with sparkling diamonds in her nose and ears, she looks all ready to go out. But instead, she is cooking milk. For coffee. Like most Indian women, my mother does not wear an apron while cooking. I guess cooks in the West get spattered all over because they know an apron will protect them. In all these years I have never seen one little speck of mustard seed sticking to my mother's blouses or a blob of turmeric staining her sari. It is indeed an art form and sensual display how an Indian woman maneuvers in a sari, in the kitchen, floating gracefully, stirring and mixing.

My mother has located her favorite stainless-steel vessel and places it on the gas stove, filled with milk. She points out that it is important for the milk to not stay stagnant for too long because the fat has a tendency to separate. Milk in India is pasteurized but not homogenized. "Stir slowly, in one direction, with a deep spoon," my mother explains. "You want to make sure the skin does not form." Every few minutes she scoops a spoonful of milk and pours it back, churning and frothing it. "This aeration process helps milk develop a creamier taste, or at least that is what South Indians believe," says my mother, who insists upon the creamiest of milk for her coffee. The sweet aroma of steaming milk begins to rise and fill the kitchen. I know we are almost there and my patience is finally going to be rewarded.

My mother pours some of her decoction into a stainless-steel glass specially designed for serving South Indian coffee. Almost immediately she spoons in the boiling milk, enough to turn the decoction light, and some sugar. I like Indian granular sugar, which is much sweeter and dissolves very slowly. I reach for a *demera*, a straight-sided and lipped bowl, and hold it steadily while she places the glass with coffee in it. I lift the glass and pour the coffee in the *demera* and then back into the glass. I repeat this several times to cool and aerate, until the coffee is frothy and mellow.

We sip our coffee slowly, sitting at the dining table, savoring every little drop. Then it is time to catch up on relatives, my friends and hers. I learn that she is helping one to secure admission into a teachers' training college, and another she is tutoring, free of charge, to help pass an English proficiency exam, and yet another, in the U.S.A., to find shelter away from an abusive home. She has set aside money to educate children with her help and many others around the country too poor and insecure to help themselves. An amazingly strong person of character, perseverance, and generosity, my mother almost instantly inspires and empowers anyone who comes in contact with her. She is not a rich woman of material wealth, but oh so rich within as she gives of herself. A beautiful woman of eighty-six, Padma Ranganathan, mother of four very fortunate daughters, is still creating and perfecting the recipe of food and life. An eternal optimist—true Renaissance woman!

The chirping of the birds is getting louder on the terrace garden and the sun rays are beginning to flow in, slowly flooding my mother's kitchen and dining room. I have had my coffee, and I am now warm all over.

Coldspot

Christina Orchid

In the early years of the 1950s, our house was a model of family efficiency. Our little Coldspot refrigerator, the center of our suburban world, was symbolic of this life. It was crammed to the nines with my mother's homemade tomato sauce, jams, jellies, pickles, sauerkraut, chutneys, and chili; tubs of lard; and concoctions for curing coughs and bringing down fevers. I longed for the after-school Cokes and brownies I was introduced to in the homes of my friends, but instead my parents warned me about the evils of tooth decay and told me to eat an apple for a snack. They scrimped on things at home to save money no matter what.

While my father drove his Studebaker into Portland every day, my mother stayed home. Intelligent and resourceful, she had grown up on a ranch and knew how to use, reuse, and make the best of everything. While she didn't drive, she could cook and sew, and she had fractious and detailed ideas about cleaning and household maintenance. I was her unwilling apprentice, and at her elbow I learned the domestic skills that were an important part of the education of all young ladies.

I was assigned a variety of tasks. It was never anything fun or good like making cookies. Instead, I'd grind bread crumbs, clamping the contraption to the counter and spending an hour cranking the machine while the dust of old dried bread my mother kept in a pan under the oven would slowly drift into the shallow bowl. In summer I dreaded the days I would find the flats of strawberries stacked in the breezeway or come into the house and see all the furniture crammed into the kitchen, the floors ready for waxing. While my friends explored the nearby woods, I would be at the sink hulling the berries while my mother readied the jars, or on my hands and knees polishing the floor with a small cloth while Mom stood over me and pointed to the spots that needed elbow grease.

My mother's relentless and exacting cooking methodology could rival that of any *Michelin* chef. No seeds, no skins, no little bones, only big ones. Tender not tough, light but not too flaky, moist not wet, browned not black, crusty not hard, buttery not greasy, sweetened slightly but not sickeningly, smooth not lumpy, creamy instead of gooey, fresh not frozen: all were culinary values my mother demanded be met in her kitchen, come hell or high water. By the time I was twelve I was convinced my mother was some kind of crackpot and railed silently as I removed every eye from every potato with the tip of the peeler. My friends said my mother was really strict. She said she had a standard and, by god, we were all going to live up to it.

As we grew, houses were built around us. Trees were planted, and our neighborhood was filled with cars and bikes. On our street everybody's dad had been in the war and we all knew where. When you first met a new kid, the standard question was "Where was your dad stationed?" The Haases were from Estonia. My friend Gregor Rose's family was Polish. They had a knitting machine in their garage that Mr. Rose had brought home from Jantzen, where he was a janitor. His wife made baby clothes on it. Gregor's older brother, Beryl, and my older brother, Bill, took turns relentlessly teasing Gregor and me.

The Roses had been in the camps (I didn't know what that meant at the time), and Mrs. Rose had a row of numbers tattooed on her forearm. My mother told me not to stare and to never say a word about those numbers. The words "survivor" and "holocaust" were years away then. Later I would realize it wasn't just the Roses; it was a whole street of survivors.

Growing up, Gregor and I vowed we would never smoke cigarettes and drink coffee like our staid mothers. We would race through the kitchen past the Coldspot, leaving them chatting in the haze of smoke, ignoring their shouted cautions to behave ourselves, to get on our bikes and get out of there.

I was in eighth grade when Gregor died of leukemia. He had been going to Hebrew school and we had already begun to drift apart, but it was still a loss. Things changed even more after that: the Roses moved away, and my parents tightened the screws further. One pair of shoes and no ski trips, and the Disneyland vacations and Hawaii spring breaks of my friends were impossible dreams.

By this time I was developing my own ideas about where I wanted to be and what I wanted to do and those ideas did not coincide in any way with my parents' stultifying and gracious life. I longed for travel to places I imagined to be sophisticated and wanted to spend my time in coffeehouses and art galleries where I would meet other "misunderstood geniuses" like myself. My new high school friends shared my interests and we carefully plotted our escape from our parents, the suburbs, and Oregon—nowheresville. The rural backwater where my parents spent their time and their money was a tiresome bore that I planned on disowning as soon as possible.

By the time I was in college I was spending holidays with schoolmates who went home to New York and San Francisco and spending less time with my parents. I was meeting lots of people—mostly guys. When my folksinger boyfriend morphed into an electrified rock 'n' roller, we moved to L.A. I got a job at Scandia as a waitress, but when I showed the new pantry kid how to peel a tomato (at a customer's request) the big Swede in charge of the kitchen begged me to come to work in the kitchen. I declined but showed him how to clean a Dungeness crab, anyway. Waiting tables was where the money was, and it didn't interfere with my party-girl life. I still had no idea that anything I had learned at home was of value.

By the time I got to New York I wasn't just working in good restaurants, I was dining in them, too. I was an exotic, "the Oregon girl" on the arm of a boy-millionaire record producer. I started to learn about champagne. In London I wore my cowboy boots and hung out with a rock star. In Geneva I fell hard for a dark-haired attorney who wore a fur coat and had houses in Montreux and Ibiza. His mother scolded me for making an omelet in the kitchen at midnight, demanding that the next time I wake the cook. I was in way over my head. When we were married at a hotel in Marrakech, I called my folks on the telephone to let them know but didn't invite them. It was the beginning of the end. Or so I thought. It was, instead, the real beginning.

Four years later I returned to the States, dumped, broke, and with a toddler in tow. My parents had retired to the San Juan Islands by then, and since I didn't have anyplace else to go I joined them. I went to work as a waitress right away and swore off men. I discovered I enjoyed taking care of my little cabin and making meals for my little boy. My mother had a huge garden, and when she handed me a paper bag full of fresh corn and ripe tomatoes I felt a rush of expectation and excitement. Within two years I had opened my own restaurant.

I didn't think I knew enough to cook, so I hired a cook and went to work in the dining room. When I complained about the presentation of some scallops, the cook walked off in a huff. I walked into the kitchen and opened the refrigerator.

It was like falling down a rabbit hole. I lived in the moment, working crisis to crisis. The kitchen became my empire. I ruled over it like a lord. I knew exactly where every hunk of cheese, bacon end, and leftover cup of lamb stock was in my vast refrigerator. My bottles and jars of vinegars and fruit compotes were not to be messed with. I found myself inspecting the dining room every day before we opened, looking for splashed butter on the walls, threads hanging from the linens. More than once I had to show the house steward how to clean the bathroom. He didn't know what elbow grease was.

I ran into Beryl Rose, my friend Gregor's brother, working at the Mexican restaurant down the street. He was the best waiter there and people loved him. He knew all the locals, had a great laugh and an excellent work ethic. I hired him on the spot. I began to relax a little when he was in the dining room, and I trusted him, so he started doing the deposit at the end of

the night. Soon it was the two of us closing the restaurant together. After a long and harrowing night in the kitchen, I
needed to do something, so we would go shoot a game of pool
before we headed off in separate directions. I didn't know
much about him except that he played softball, and his wife,
the belly dancer, had left him for an astrologer. We were just
friends. We were still just friends several months later when in
the throes of a breakdown (the bank was pressing hard), I accepted an invitation for a glass of wine at his house. After two
glasses I ended up pouring my wretched, almost-defeated heart
out. While I sobbed, he put his arms around me and told me
not to worry, everything would be all right.

The next morning I stood in his shower for a good ten minutes enveloped in steam and a sense of well-being. When I
went to the kitchen, I had a surprise. There, in the room, was
my family's old refrigerator from Oregon. Beryl had bought it
from my parents. It turned out they were well acquainted.
When I saw him from the backside, opening the door to the
familiar Coldspot, the dark curls damp at his neck, a wave of
tenderness washed over me. He made me a breakfast of tortillas and eggs.

During this time, I was cooking every day. My mother began leaving plastic buckets of cut herbs and boxes of strange
things at her gate for me to pick up on my way to work. The
sorrel she gave me made the restaurant's salmon something of

a wonder and the kohlrabies went into a soup with mustard and leeks. I had to call my mother to find out what they were. She just laughed when I said they looked like dirt clods. Adding mustard to the soup was her idea.

The nightly cleaning ritual in the restaurant's kitchen had become like a Zen meditation for me. No matter how hot, tired, and burned I was, I took my time. Every night I scoured the sink with cleanser, rinsed it, and then scrubbed around the base of the faucets with an old toothbrush. When I showed the dishwasher how to clean around the faucets with the brush, he stood silent and amazed as all the black crud disappeared from around their bases, the line where the chrome and porcelain met gleaming and new again. The jolt of happiness I experienced was sheer pleasure. Exhausted, with red welts on the backs of my hands, I was happy. I was doing exactly what I was meant to do. I liked cooking, I liked feeding people, I liked amazing my staff with my arcane knowledge. In a flash I realized my entire life experience had led me to this moment, cleaning the sink perfectly and beautifully at 1 A.M. on an island off the coast of Washington State in my very own restaurant's kitchen.

It was another eight years before I married Beryl Rose. And another eight before I gave him the checkbook and the password. He was very patient. We built our restaurant together and whatever other plans he had, he set aside to help me follow my dream.

Twenty-five years ago, when I stepped into the kitchen to cover for my disappeared cook, chefs were not celebrities, and restaurants were more likely to have a famous maître d' and a nameless kitchen crew. Today, TV, books, and magazines are as important for chefs and restaurants as comfortable chairs and good bread. My mother likes to infer that she saw it all coming, that she knew she was training me for an important career. The truth is, I would never have been successful without the rebellious spirit, the desire for adventure, and the fearlessness that sprouted in reaction to my regimented and safe childhood. It is also true that the domestic skills I learned at home, like a forced march, were invaluable lessons as well, but without the attitude I would have been just another really good cook.

My forays into books and TV are just enough to keep me in business, and I am always happy when I return to my kitchen on the waterfront where I still cook a few nights a week. My mother is eighty-seven and still out in her garden. When she hands me a bucket of tomatoes, she says, "You know how to peel these, don't you?" I want to say, "Mom, I have peeled more tomatoes than you will ever know." But her face is straight, and there is only a slight twinkle in her gaze, and I realize this is now a joke between us, like the battery-powered submersible scrub brush I got her for Mother's Day. So I give it back to her, deadpan, the old saw, "Yeah, I know how to peel 'em, my mama didn't raise no nitwit." She winces at the bad grammar, but I get a laugh, too.

The Coldspot sits in Beryl's and my pantry, and when my mom and the grandkids visit with their parents we fill it with Cokes and root beer, apple juice and bacon, potato salad and brownies, macaroni and cheese and watermelon, and some real French champagne to toast our good luck.

Food Before Sanity

Lela Nargi

I recently fired my therapist. Actually, to be honest, in the last eight months I have fired two therapists. I fired the first one after she recommended a novel to me—her "new favorite," she said—that was so trite, so poorly written, that, as much as it pained me, I had to admit I'd lost all respect for her. Call this firing a simple case of literary snobbery, then. As for the second therapist, I fired her for a slightly more complicated reason. I fired her because she insisted on talking about food.

I should explain first of all that I am not overweight. I am not now, nor have I ever been, anorexic, bulimic, or even anemic. I never thought of myself as a person with "food issues." Look at my childhood, an idyll of cookery. An average day found my mother in the kitchen, flitting from fridge to stove to cabinets. With great competence and no small amount of panache, she could stir the contents of a pot, shake a skillet, season something freshly ladled from the pressure cooker, toss a salad, and remove two loaves of bread to cool on a wire rack with hands padded by lobsterlike oven mitts. On my birthday, she would decorate a three-tiered cake with elaborate piping and lavender-icing flowers she spent a whole day coaxing through a decorator's tube, petal by petal. On other special occasions, she let me thumb through her cookbooks and pick the menu. My favorite was the Japanese cookbook, a folio of large cards with recipes in both English and Japanese on one side, photos of the finished dish on the other. In the photos all the food looked like treasure: carrots were carved like swans, slices of fish were rolled like roses, grains of rice gleamed like seed pearls. "Food is magic," the book seemed to whisper. And I believed it.

I believe it even now. Every summer Saturday finds me at the farmers' market, gasping in disbelief at the sights and smells of overabundance. How to choose from forty varieties of lettuce? The intoxicating scent of peaches is so potent that I can follow it, past the fragrant melons and the explosively sweet-smelling cherries, all the way to the stall at the far end of the market.

Then there is the taste of a truly fresh egg, subtle and buttery. It is my gladdening companion through a forty-five-minute wait on a farm-stand line. Other marketers pass as I wait along with sixty or more like-minded egg lovers.

"Wow, look at this line," the passersby marvel. "What are you all waiting for?"

"Eggs," we say, smirking, waiting for the unvarying response of: "*Eggs!*" A shake of the head, a bemused frown, a muttering to a companion as the disbeliever wanders away from the line: "They're waiting for *eggs!*"

Of course what the disbelievers do not know, what everyone waiting on line *does* know, is that we are not really waiting for eggs. We are waiting for a vessel of suspended disbelief: a taste that will satisfy beyond our wildest imaginings, make us catch our breath, then groan in amazement; a vehicle that will transport us beyond the world of "eggs" and into the far superior kingdom of "Eggs!" A tomato can be such a vessel, too; so can a chocolate cake. This is why food is magic. It holds infinite, unprecedented delights, never exhausted.

People don't believe that I eat much. I am skinny, have lived my whole life as a skinny person. Consequently, I have lived with scorn. People don't seem to hold much stock in the positive powers of genetics. My mother is skinny, so was my father, so are all my cousins and grandparents. People don't consider this proof. I can almost hear their brains grinding over meatier possibilities: a family of bulimics, a family addicted to painkillers, a whole family infected with a rare stomach disease. Sometimes I let people off the hook with a lie, tell them we are a family of alcoholic chain-smokers, and watch as their faces are consumed by relief.

Nor do people believe me when I say that I don't really care much for junk food. They test me: French fries? Potato chips? Cheez Doodles? Doritos? Hostess cupcakes? Mallomars? M&M's? Listen, I tell them, I'm a person who will follow my nose three blocks to get a bushel of peaches. Candy, snack foods, they hardly rate by comparison. I've been this way since I was a girl; at the age of seven I braved cafeteria taunts in order to eat niçoise olives and my beloved lupini beans with lunch. I knew nothing then about junk food. This was because my mother shunned Snickers in favor of figs and homemade peanut butter; her pots and pans were never disgraced by the addition of packaged mac and cheese, or canned ravioli.

Having brought up my mother for the third time now, maybe I should draw this excursus back around to where I began, with my therapist. My therapist, naturally, was always keen to link my every motive, my every small utterance to my mother. Our last conversation, two days before I left her a cowardly phone message explaining that we were through for good, was no exception. A reenactment:

SHE: Let's talk about food today.
ME (*Puzzled*): Um, okay.

SHE: How do you feel about food?

ME: How do I feel about food? What do you mean?

SHE: Do you like food? Do you hate food? Are you ambiva-
lent about food? *What does food mean to you?*

ME: Uh, I guess you could say I love food. I love to cook. I
love to eat. . . .

SHE: Interesting . . . What do you love to eat?

ME: Gee, I don't know. All kinds of things.

SHE: You must be more specific.

Let me interrupt this scintillating dialogue for a moment to
explain that by the time this conversation is taking place I
have already been suspecting, for a number of weeks, that my
therapist is not a food-lover. She barely batted an eyelash on
my first visit, when I told her I'd published a cookbook; a food-
lover, even a professionally disengaged psychotherapist
food-lover, would want to know more. In her office, a faint
aroma of garlic, or apples, or any giveaways as to what was in-
gested for lunch, never lingers. Therapists eat at their desks—
quickly, granted, but you'd think some lunch smell would
stick—and the chronic, unvarying scent of carpet and hot
lightbulbs in my therapist's office makes me think perhaps she
does not even like the smell of food. Finally, my hunch: she
just doesn't look like the kind of person who cooks. I can't
imagine her juggling spices, or grease-splattering her kitchen.

She is definitely takeout material. What do you tell a person like this when they ask you what you like to eat, especially when you're the kind of person who waits forty-five minutes in line to buy fresh eggs?

> ME: I like just about everything, any good food. I can't pick favorites.
>
> SHE: What *don't* you like to eat?
>
> ME: Turnips. Oh, and I don't like cooked peppers mixed into a dish, although on their own they're fine. And I'm not overly fond of the taste of bergamot.
>
> SHE (*Looking exasperated but determined not to ask me what bergamot is*): Let's try this another way. What do you normally eat for breakfast?
>
> ME: Well, except on weekends I don't spend a lot of time on breakfast. Usually, I just eat toast, or a banana. I like to eat quickly so I can get to my desk and start working.
>
> SHE (*Looking delighted, like she might actually utter the word "Aha!"*): Ahhh . . . so you hate to eat breakfast.

To interject again: how do you explain to someone who is not a food-lover that if you are the kind of person who likes all flavors except turnip and bergamot, you might also be the kind of person who really enjoys a plain banana when it is perfectly ripe, with a firm texture and no brown spots; that, in fact, you can hardly imagine a better breakfast because this one really does it for you, really satisfies?

> ME (*Trapped into virtual non sequitur*): Actually, I love bananas.
>
> SHE: But you don't like toast. . . .
>
> ME: (*Confused silence*)
>
> SHE: What about your childhood? Did your mother cook?
>
> ME: My mother was a fabulous cook. She made gourmet five-course dinners every night, and that was in addition to going to work, taking care of me, doing all the shopping, and cleaning up.
>
> SHE: And your father did *nothing*?
>
> ME: That's right.
>
> SHE: Did your mother actually *like* to cook?
>
> ME: Well, yes. My father may have been a domineering jerk who never lifted a finger around the house, but he never forced my mother to make bouillabaisse, or Peking duck, or coq au vin. He would have eaten any swill she served up. She cooked these things because she liked to cook them.
>
> SHE: Hmmmmm. And now you like to cook. That's interesting. How did you feel as a girl when your mother would make these elaborate meals? How did it make you feel about your father?

And here I will leave off the dialogue. If it wasn't bad enough that we were going to talk (again) about my mother, adding my father to the mix was really deflating my desire to "discover" anything about my relationship with food (a relationship, I learned at the end of our session, my therapist had been convinced was based on anorexia, since I'm so skinny). Because what does the above conversation really conjure? An unhappy American family circa 1973, with a father who does no housework, a mother who does all the cooking, two parents who still accept—it is 1973, after all, the year almost no one imagined Billie Jean King could trounce flabby Bobby Riggs in a so-called Battle of the Sexes—that in most American households this is normal. (Of course, it was somewhat less normal in 1978, when my mother finally left my father, thereby joining the legions of divorced single mothers who no longer had the time or the stamina to prepare five-course dinners.) Really, there is only one circumstance in this brief plunge into my childhood that someone might consider slightly out of the ordinary, and that is that my mother was a mighty and accomplished cook.

People who do not cook are suspicious of this talent in others.

I learned to cook from my mother. When I say "learned," I don't mean that she gave me lessons, or even that I spent much time watching her in the kitchen. I learned to cook by recognizing my mother's love for food. This I learned through osmosis, as I learned to react to an annoying bit of news by watching how my mother tightened her lips slightly and let her eyes go blank. And as I learned to be afraid to sing in public, because she is. Daughters learn plenty of things from their mothers without even wanting to. Not all these things are stimulating fodder worthy of the cost of a visit to the psychotherapist's office.

My mother's love of food was palpable, inspiring. She would hunker down with her cookbooks, giving them a good going-over every now and again as if she were rereading a favorite novel. She liked to pick up strange foodstuffs in the supermarkets to experiment with: In 1973, dried poblano peppers were exotic; so was eel. Her eyes would take on a confident, conquering spark when she contemplated the tidy row of fruits and vegetables at the greengrocer's, coming to rest on the plumpest, the most inevitably delicious.

My mother was all concentration when she cooked; nothing could distract her. She wore in the kitchen an expression of intense calm. Not every new dish was a triumph, but she never second-guessed herself, never lost confidence. The kitchen is the only place where I've seen her approach joy. In the kitchen she was completely absorbed, absolutely herself.

These things I say about my mother—most of them, now, also apply to me. Like my mother, I love food and all things related to it.

I fired my therapist because she didn't love food. I suppose you could say this was petty. But a person who does not love food cannot understand the propensity in others, cannot feel empathy for their disposition. They do not realize that, for a food-lover, to draw food into the realm of "issues" and family is to ruin its magic forever. By the age of twenty, all daughters know they are like their mothers, and all daughters wish they were less so. By the age of thirty, most daughters are exhausted by the prospect of another ten years of battling the onslaught of motherlike tendencies. With a sigh, we resign ourselves to any number of cringe-worthy similarities. Positive associations we admit quietly.

I learned to love food through my mother, maybe even—so throw a bone to therapists—in spite of my mother. Purely within the context of eating and food, it does not matter to me that my father never did the grocery shopping. Or that my mother, perhaps, used elaborate cookery as a way to gain some distance, as a way to remove herself for hours at a time from the daily drudgery of her wifely and motherly existence.

From my mother, too, I learned to love cooking. I do not want to question why I love to cook. Would it really matter if I did so in order to gain my mother's approval? Or because I had some deep-seated need to take care of people? Or to satisfy my ego? To love food, and to love to cook—why should I want to analyze these loves away?

Some evenings at dinnertime, I catch myself flitting around my own kitchen in mindful oblivion, and recognize my mother in action. I take a brief moment to settle into this concordance, standing there amid the cheerful detritus of another night's cooking experiment—spills of saffron and cumin, a few dirty spoons, stove-top splatters of every shape and color—and imagine how my ex-therapist would balk at the scene.

> SHE: You mean to tell me that you just let the sauce *bubble over* like that, all over the kitchen, and didn't even clean it up?
>
> ME: Yes. Then, after I ate my meal straight out of the pot, I let the dog lick sauce off my chin. She's always been a big fan of my cooking.

The Queen of Mold

Ruth Reichl

This is a true story.

Imagine a New York City apartment at six in the morning. It is a modest apartment in Greenwich Village. Coffee is bubbling in an electric percolator. On the table is a basket of rye bread, an entire coffee cake, a few cheeses, a platter of cold cuts. My mother has been making breakfast—a major meal in our house, one where we sit down to fresh orange juice every morning, clink our glasses as if they held wine, and toast each other with "Cheerio. Have a nice day."

Right now she is the only one awake, but she is getting impatient for the day to begin and she cranks WQXR up a little louder on the radio, hoping that the noise will rouse everyone else. But Dad and I are good sleepers, and when the sounds of martial music have no effect she barges into the bedroom and shakes my father awake.

"Darling," she says, "I need you. Get up and come into the kitchen."

My father, a sweet and accommodating person, shuffles sleepily down the hall. He is wearing loose pajamas, and the strand of hair he combs over his bald spot stands straight up. He leans against the sink, holding on to it a little, and obediently opens his mouth when my mother says, "Try this."

Later, when he told the story, he attempted to convey the awfulness of what she had given him. The first time he said that it tasted like cat toes and rotted barley, but over the years the description got better. Two years later it had turned into pigs' snouts and mud, and five years later he had refined the flavor into a mixture of antique anchovies and moldy chocolate.

Whatever it tasted like, he said it was the worst thing he had ever had in his mouth, so terrible that it was impossible to swallow, so terrible that he leaned over and spit it into the sink and then grabbed the coffeepot, put the spout into his mouth, and tried to eradicate the flavor.

My mother stood there watching all this. When my father finally put the coffeepot down, she smiled and said, "Just as I thought. Spoiled."

And then she threw the mess into the garbage can and sat down to drink her orange juice.

For the longest time I thought I had made this story up. But my brother insists that my father told it often, and with a certain amount of pride. As far as I know, my mother was never embarrassed by the telling, never even knew that she should have been. It was just the way she was.

Which was taste-blind and unafraid of rot. "Oh, it's just a little mold," I can remember her saying on the many occasions she scraped the fuzzy blue stuff off some concoction before serving what was left for dinner. She had an iron stomach and was incapable of understanding that other people did not.

This taught me many things. The first was that food could be dangerous, especially to those who loved it. I took this very seriously. My parents entertained a great deal, and before I was ten I had appointed myself guardian of the guests. My mission was to keep Mom from killing anybody who came to dinner.

Her friends seemed surprisingly unaware that they took their lives in their hands each time they ate with us. They chalked their ailments up to the weather, the flu, or one of my mother's more unusual dishes. "No more sea urchins for me," I imagined Burt Langner saying to his wife, Ruth, after a dinner at our house, "they just don't agree with me." Little did he know that it was not the sea urchins that had made him ill, but that bargain beef my mother had found so irresistible.

"I can make a meal out of anything," Mom told her friends proudly. She liked to brag about "Everything Stew," a dish invented while she was concocting a casserole out of a two-week-old turkey carcass. (The very fact that my mother confessed to cooking with two-week-old turkey says a lot about her.) She put the turkey and a half can of mushroom soup into the pot. Then she began rummaging around in the refrigerator. She found some leftover broccoli and added that. A few carrots went in, and then a half carton of sour cream. In a hurry, as usual, she added green beans and cranberry sauce. And then, somehow, half an apple pie slipped into the dish. Mom looked momentarily horrified. Then she shrugged and said, "Who knows? Maybe it will be good." And she began throwing everything in the refrigerator in along with it—leftover pâté, some cheese ends, a few squishy tomatoes.

That night I set up camp in the dining room. I was particularly worried about the big eaters, and I stared at my favorite people as they approached the buffet, willing them away from the casserole. I actually stood directly in front of Burt Langner so he couldn't reach the turkey disaster. I loved him, and I knew that he loved food.

Unknowingly I had started sorting people by their tastes.

Like a hearing child born to deaf parents, I was shaped by my mother's handicap, discovering that food could be a way of making sense of the world.

At first I paid attention only to taste, storing away the knowledge that my father preferred salt to sugar and my mother had a sweet tooth. Later I also began to note how people ate, and where. My brother liked fancy food in fine surroundings, my father only cared about the company, and Mom would eat anything so long as the location was exotic. I was slowly discovering that if you watched people as they ate, you could find out who they were.

Then I began listening to the way people talked about food, looking for clues to their personalities. "What is she really saying?" I asked myself when Mom bragged about the invention of her famous corned beef ham.

"I was giving a party," she'd begin, "and as usual I left everything for the last minute." Here she'd look at her audience, laughing softly at herself. "I asked Ernst to do the shopping, but you know how absentminded he is! Instead of picking up a ham, he brought me corned beef." She'd look pointedly at Dad, who would look properly sheepish.

"What could I do?" Mom asked. "I had people coming in a couple of hours. I had no choice. I simply pretended it was a ham." With that, Dad would look admiringly at my mother, pick up his carving knife, and start serving the masterpiece.

MIRIAM REICHL'S CORNED BEEF HAM

4 pounds whole corned beef

5 bay leaves

1 onion, chopped

1 tablespoon prepared mustard

¼ cup brown sugar

Whole cloves

1 can (1 pound 15 oz.) spiced peaches

Cover corned beef with water in a large pot. Add bay leaves and onion. Cook over medium heat about 3 hours, until meat is very tender.

While meat is cooking, mix mustard and brown sugar.

Preheat oven to 325°F.

Take meat from water and remove all visible fat. Insert cloves into meat as if it were ham. Cover the meat with the mustard mixture and bake 1 hour, basting frequently with the peach syrup.

Surround meat with spiced peaches and serve.

Serves 6.

Pastelitos and Memories

Kitty Morse

I was filled with happy anticipation on this sunny morning. Tante Suzanne, my great-aunt, better known to us as Tita, had agreed to teach me how to make *pastelitos*.

Along the Boulevard de la Gare, Casablanca's pulsating central artery, I joined the colorful crowd of men in robelike *gandouras*, businessmen in suits, and women in hooded *djellabahs* walking arm in arm with teenagers wearing jeans. Casablanca always struck me as schizophrenic, incapable of making its mind up between the veil or the miniskirt. Since my departure for the United States when I was in my teens, my hometown evolved from a picturesque port city aptly named "White House," to a jumble of minarets and sleek office towers emerging from a tide of unregulated traffic.

The buildings fronting the boulevard always reminded me of photographs of downtown Havana. Tears of grime streaked ornate Moorish art deco facades, as if the decrepit buildings mourned faded glories. This was still home, nonetheless, and it was good to be back, if only for a visit, and steep myself in familiar territory.

My excitement increased as I neared Tita's apartment. The crisp little phyllo triangles we called *pastelitos* were the hit of every family gathering, and like many cooks of her generation, Tita wasn't one to part easily with a recipe. From the street, I noticed one of Casa's ubiquitous pigeons perched atop the winged cherub that adorned the rim of Tita's dining-room balcony. The stone figurine, once a quaint decorative accent, was now just an antiquated reminder of the architectural style popular under the French Protectorate. The building's interior, however, with its graceful iron railings, intricate plasterwork, and curving marble staircase, still showed remnants of its original art deco grandeur. As I climbed up the damp stairs, the odor of *Eau de Javel* bleach followed me to the fourth floor. I remembered the family code and pressed Tita's doorbell briefly three times. Fatima answered. The aging housemaid had been in Tita's employ ever since I could remember.

"*Labess! Bonjour!* Madame Suzanne, she is in the kitchen, as usual," said the kindly Fatima, flashing a new gold tooth.

The copper-skinned servant released me from a musk-scented embrace, and invited me to follow her as she padded down the corridor, the panels of her kaftan swelling to the rhythm of her wide hips. The soles of her feet were colored bright orange from henna, a common practice among Moroccan women, to soften the skin. Along the walls, photographs of my ancestors seemed to follow me with their gaze. I recognized my grandfather Pépé, Tita's brother, dressed in a young boy's sailor shirt and knee-highs. He looked at me with pensive eyes, his arm resting nonchalantly on his toy hoop. The picture gallery lent Tita's apartment a museumlike quality, but the rainbow of scents emanating from the kitchen dispelled any thought of the past.

"*Ma chérie!* I am so happy to see you!" exclaimed the queen of this fragrant domain.

The contrast between the long, cavernous hallway and the youthful pitch of Tita's voice was striking. She was rinsing a bunch of parsley in the sink. She turned around just long enough for me to plant a sonorous kiss on both her cheeks. As a child, I feared that her skin, so delicate as to be almost transparent, would dissolve under the pressure of my lips. As usual, she wore a fashionable black dress over her tiny, five-foot frame, a strand of pearls, and black leather pumps. Slightly drooping eyelids accented her wistful gray eyes framed in a halo of snow-white hair. Tita wasn't one to dwell on nostalgia, however. Her sunny disposition fooled many into thinking that she was much younger than her seventy-five years. I couldn't remember a single conversation with my great-aunt when the subject didn't turn to food. For us, this common passion forged the bond that straddled generations.

"Ready for our lesson?"

"Yes! I even brought measuring cups from America!" I exclaimed.

She cast a quick look at my implements, and just as quickly, dismissed them. Using cups and tablespoons seemed unnecessary to one who measured ingredients in half an eggshell, a mint tea glass, or a yogurt container. "What kind of cook needs to know exact amounts? I measure everything with my eyes!"

Like many North African cooks, she clung to the time-honored Moroccan principle of *eenek mi zanek* (Let your eyes be your guide). She had also been known to omit an ingredient or two, on purpose. Thus, when she offered to divulge the real recipe for her prized *pastelitos*, I jumped at the chance. My challenge would be to make her pause long enough to ascertain the equivalent of her "pinches" of cumin, or of a glass of diced onion, in tablespoons and measuring cups. To do that, I appealed to her sense of pride.

"If I don't know the exact amounts, how will my readers make *pastelitos* as good as yours?"

She looked at me with a touch of condescension.

"Ah, *oui*. I forgot, American cooks, they like to measure exactly."

Tita's kitchen, like its owner, radiated the warm patina that comes from decades of nurturing. The diminutive space was her stage, and she, the director. I was thrilled to be the privileged apprentice, if only for a short while.

Copper pots polished to a mirrorlike sheen dangled above my great-aunt's head. A bulging straw *couffin* overflowing with leafy bouquets of coriander and parsley were proof that she had already gone to the Marché Centrale, Casablanca's covered central market. On the small wooden table, two kilos of *warka* leaves, the phyllolike circles of dough necessary to make *pastelitos*, were tucked under a damp towel. In true Tita style, there appeared to be enough for an army. A new bottle of Butagaz butane was wedged between the stove and the refrigerator. The stage was set for our lesson.

I was wrapping an apron around my waist when the doorbell rang. Fatima padded to the door once again.

"I hope it's not Leah," said Tita, rolling her eyes. "You know how nosy she is."

The click of high heels announced that it was indeed Leah, Tita's upstairs neighbor. As usual, she was drenched in florid *Maja Myrurgia* perfume, and made up like a store mannequin, her white bangs smoothed just so above her eyebrows to set off her aquamarine eyes. She reminded me of Norma Desmond in

Sunset Boulevard, always ready for her close-up. Leah, it was clear, relished center stage.

Fatima squatted anew on the terrazzo floor and resumed peeling garlic cloves. Her eye caught mine, as if to warn: "Sparks are going to fly!"

Tita forced a smile. "*Bonjour*, Leah. What a nice surprise," she said, a little too sweetly.

I knew her well enough to sense that she wished Leah would simply turn on her heels and go home. Instead, the two exchanged air kisses.

"The concierrrrge told Akika that the *Amerrrrikiya* just arrived. What arrre you making, chérrrie?" Leah asked, diamond rings flashing.

The native Spanish speaker had never mastered the more guttural French. She rolled her *r*'s around her tongue like an opera singer.

"I'm showing Katy how to make *pastelitos*," said Tita over the splash of running water. Like my hometown, I too suffered from a split personality. My French-speaking friends and relatives always called me Katy (Kah-ty), while the rest of the world knew me as "Kitty."

"Everyone's crrrazy about my *pastelitos*!" Leah interrupted. "You want to include them in your book as well?"

My interest in recording family recipes wasn't lost on Tita's neighbor. I had an inkling her visit was not serendipitous; her tendency to grab the limelight was well known.

"I'm sure Katy can learn a thing or two from you, as well!" I thought Tita's voice denoted an edge of testiness. "Why don't you join us?"

With crimson claws, Leah nonchalantly lifted a leaf of the paper-thin *warka* from the stack on the table, and held it up for inspection.

"Where did you get these rrrounds?" she asked. "They don't look thin enough to me."

"I hired Asmah to make them. She was here yesterday," Tita retorted.

Asmah was renowned for producing rounds as thin as onionskin. The painstaking process of making *warka* over a charcoal fire, using the special *tobsil dial warka*, copper pan, took years of experience. The old woman was so adept at the task that she could turn out a kilo of paper-thin leaves in under an hour. Experts like Asmah were scarce.

"I think Asmah is losing her touch," continued Leah, ignoring my great-aunt's feelings. "You know, Suzanne, the *pastelitos* you served last week, I thought they were a little tough. Maybe it was Asmah's *warrrka*. I use the commercial one from the *marché*, why don't you?"

The flippant tone of Leah's voice didn't sit well with Tita.

"It's fresh *warka* that makes *pastelitos* so crispy," she replied. "I never use store-bought rounds. Not when I can hire Asmah."

My great-aunt started reducing a bunch of parsley to a mound of minced leaves. To my ears, the staccato of her knife sounded more forceful than necessary.

"See how finely I mince the parsley? Come here and look," she demanded.

I complied and jotted her advice in my notebook.

"No, no, not like that," interjected our perfumed intruder, gold bracelets jangling. "Coarrrsely chopped. That's the secrrret. Yourrr pastelitos, they needed a bit more texturrre. Maybe you shouldn't chop the herrrbs so fine. Here, look at me," she added for my benefit.

She cut off the stems from a bunch of fresh coriander and sliced through the leaves, turning out thin little ribbons. It was obvious she lacked the skills that Tita practiced so effortlessly.

"Suzanne, I'm telling you, this is the way to give *pastelitos* more flavor. This is the size I like," declared Leah, casting a satisfied look at the green mound in front of her.

"No, no," exclaimed Tita with growing impatience. "The herbs must be very fine. You wrote that down, *hein?*" she insisted, verifying my scribblings.

My great-aunt was exhibiting a competitive spirit that belied her normally sweet behavior. In spite of the heat, the atmosphere in the kitchen was turning as icy as the interior of the sputtering refrigerator. I sensed Tita's aggravation, and, not quite knowing what to do, I busied myself at the sink. Leah ignored us and started chopping garlic. I was trying to find words to smooth my great-aunt's feelings, when fate intervened. Leah sliced through one of her carmine nails with her chopping knife.

"My manicurrre. It is rrruined!" she wailed. "I must go home and fix it."

She set aside the knife, and without farewell, disappeared down the hallway. We heard her heels click up the stairs. Tita, still smarting from her neighbor's criticism, brushed away a stray lock of wispy white hair.

"How dare she criticize the way I cook! She can't even hold a knife. Her *pastelitos*, I bet she buys them ready-made, too."

The wise Fatima knew how to handle her lifelong employer.

"Akika the maid, she does most of the cooking at Madame Leah's! Your *pastelitos*, they are the best, everyone knows that!"

Fatima's words seemed to appease Tita's exasperation. My great-aunt regained her good humor and wasted no time in resuming our cooking session.

"Now, add my herbs to the ground beef. Are you writing this down?"

She paused so I could capture the "pinches" of cumin, salt, and pepper in my measuring spoons.

"Fatima! The garlic!"

Tita tossed a hillock of minced garlic into the mixture.

"Just write down two soupspoons. I know by looking it is two soupspoons."

The heaping amounts hinted to me that she may have been overgenerous with the garlic, but who was I to question the age-old practice of *eenek mi zanek*?

"Now use your hands," ordered my mentor. "That's the only way to get a feel for the right consistency."

I relegated pen and paper to the top of the refrigerator, and washed my hands. Plunging them into the ground meat, I blended the mixture into a homogeneous mass under Tita's watchful gaze. Her look softened.

"I used to help Mémé Luna, my grandmother, just like this, when I was a little girl. Sometimes she would allow your grandfather and me to stand next to her on a stool, so we could see everything that was going on. The kitchen smelled so good, especially when Mémé was getting ready for La Mimouna!"

How clearly I could picture Tita and her brother, noses level with the kitchen table, so as not to miss a beat in the action. Tita, like her grandmother, was especially fond of La Mimouna, a celebration unique to Morocco's Jews. On the last night of Passover, she followed Mémé Luna's example and opened her doors to Jewish and Muslim friends, and treated them to pyramids of crisp little *pastelitos*, exotic clove-scented *moustiniz* macaroons, addictive dates bulging with almond paste, and her exquisite *Couscous de La Mimouna* liberally sprinkled with orange blossom water.

"I wish you could have met Mémé Luna," continued my great-aunt in a dreamy tone. "We called her Mémé Luna because her face was as round as the moon."

From the photograph hanging on Tita's wall, Mémé Luna looked more like the Mother Superior in long black skirt and matching high-necked blouse, her hair hidden under a severe black scarf. In Tita's mind, however, Luna was still the loving grandmother who overlooked all kinds of mischief. My great-aunt sighed as she incorporated the sweet flavor of memories into the meat filling.

"Once, your grandfather and I, we ate so many of Mémé Luna's *pastelitos* that we caught an indigestion. Our mother got so upset!"

As she spoke, Tita's reminiscences imprinted themselves on my consciousness as well, leaving me with a warm sense of belonging to a long line of family *cuisinières*. I could almost feel them looking over my shoulder. My great-aunt cut short her musings by poking the filling and licking her index finger clean.

"Perfect! Now, let's fill the *pastelitos*."

She coached me along as I folded each round of *warka* into a half-moon shape, then into a strip about two inches wide. Patiently, she handed me one heaping spoon of the filling after another, and showed me how to place it just above the narrow edge closest to me.

"You fold the *warka* on the diagonal," she explained, pushing me gently aside to demonstrate. "That way, you have a little left for tucking inside when you reach the top, see?"

We worked quickly to prevent the paper-thin dough from drying when it came in contact with the air. Like Tita, I felt Mémé Luna's presence, as my great-aunt inserted a tongue of *warka* inside the final fold of a perfect triangle. I had to repeat the process a good half dozen times before I was able to emulate her.

"Do you know the meaning of the word *pastelitos?*" she asked, adjusting the amount of filling on the strip in front of me.

As descendants of Andalusian Jews, many on Tita's side of the family referred to certain dishes by their original Spanish names. My great-aunt, like most of her relatives, was fluent in French, Spanish, and Arabic.

"To us, *pastelitos* means 'little pastries.' But my Arab friends, they call them *briouats*, 'small letters.' It's because you never know what delicious filling is hidden inside! Just like these!"

My pastries finally passed Tita's inspection, and she instructed Fatima to fill a gleaming copper pan with vegetable oil. The antiquated gas stove wooshed to life at the lighting of a match. In minutes, the scent of frying pastries swirled around the kitchen and escaped through the open door into the common courtyard. The whole building knew instantly what we were up to.

At Tita's direction, I waited for each *pastelito* to turn a glistening amber before setting it to drain on paper towels. All of sudden, the phone rang. Tita went to answer it.

"That was Leah!" she said, reentering our fragrant haven. "She smelled the pastries when she opened her back door and she asked if Fatima could bring her a few! That Leah! She never misses a trick! We'll send her some later!"

"I told you how Madame Leah, she hates to cook!" said Fatima, breaking into peels of laughter.

Tita joined in the fun. I was contemplating the consequences of my gluttony as I put away one after the other of Tita's savory little treats, when my great-aunt gave her final assessment.

"These pastries taste almost like Mémé Luna's," she said with the concentration of a professional food critic. "Maybe I have put in too much garlic, what do you think? My eyes must be getting old. Your American measuring spoons would prevent me from making such a mistake. Can you get me a set?"

Of Wine and Men

Royal Mack

A good man is like a fine bottle of wine," Aunt Shirley says. "Don't drink bad wine and don't date bad men. Just Don't Do It." As if *not* doing something might be any easier than following a certain sportswear maker's mantra that assumes we all know what incredible, impossible thing each of us should be doing if only we'd get off our butts and *just do it*.

I am in the kitchen audibly cursing my most recent failed romance—a guy I refer to only as "the Squasher"—when Aunt Shirley, during her annual pit stop at our house en route to another far-flung adventure, pushes the door open and shares her advice.

"I'm a little angry right now, Aunt Shirley," I reply. "Maybe instead of tossing your clever quips around, you could tell me exactly how a good man is like a fine bottle of wine and how I can tell, preferably before I buy it, take it home, and get ill."

"Love to," she says, like she'd just been waiting for me to ask. Aunt Shirley has consumed a lot of wine and men, which she claims makes her an expert on both, and she's never been one to hold back on saying so.

My mom, who happens to be Aunt Shirley's twin, knew this was coming. So now she's in the kitchen, too. "Men are not bottles of wine, Shirley," she says quite seriously. "And she doesn't need any additional confusion. She certainly doesn't need advice on her love life from a twice-divorced actress!" (Mom loves her sister, but she's always been a little jealous of Aunt Shirley's wilder nature.)

I turn to my mother. "What have I got to lose? A date?"

"Exactly," says Aunt Shirley. "She might even learn something—even if it's only about wine. That alone will improve her life."

Mom rolls her eyes and turns in the direction of the laundry room. "You're on your own, honey. Don't get drunk." And with that she disappears on the other side of the swing door.

"I love your mother, but for identical twins, we couldn't be more different," Aunt Shirley says with great emotional subtext, before shooing me out of the kitchen. "Wait on the couch and prepare to learn."

I'm not sure what to expect. Whenever she talks about

wine, she carries on about Brix and appellations and other things that only wine geeks who've seen *Sideways* ten times talk about. Even if she tries to explain how men and wine are alike, I might not get it. I'm a "house wine" girl and I rarely venture outside the house. Now Aunt Shirley's aiming to change that. But at this point, judging from my lack of dating success, it seems to me that staying inside the house is just plain good sense. *Just don't do it.*

After all, I wasn't even safe at Whole Foods, where I'd met the Squasher. There he was, successful and well dressed, in the vegetable section squeezing tomatoes (a little too hard, if I'd been honest with myself). Everything seemed perfect in the beginning, but I failed to heed the signs: eyes roving around any restaurant we went to and frequent requests for me to repeat what I'd said. In retrospect, I think even the wine he chose would have preferred being at another table; maybe under the table, in the trash. But then he didn't ask for my opinion—another warning unheeded.

I should have thanked him for the time we spent together and said good night. Instead, I kept on bravely trying to turn it all around. But vinegar is not going to turn into Cheval Blanc no matter how much time you give it, and I was not going to get the tomato squasher to be an attentive friend, let alone a good date. Unfortunately, he stopped calling before I had the chance to tell him he was one bad bottle of vino.

"Here we are," says Aunt Shirley dramatically, as she whisks a tray of elegantly arranged cheese and crackers, a bowl, a pitcher of water, and two wineglasses onto the coffee table. She then opens a cabinet in my own living room and takes out a box.

"What's that?" I ask, incredulous that I was unaware of things going on in my house.

"I had a feeling this might come up and now it has. I'm going to show you how, if you listen carefully, you will avoid both bad wine and bad men."

She yanks the top off the box without damaging her French manicure—a lesson in itself—and pulls a bottle of wine from the box.

"Oh, flashy—California Zinfandel!" Aunt Shirley exclaims, showing me the bottle brandishing a particularly colorful label. "It's probably a good idea to avoid flashy men from California."

Wielding a corkscrew, she pops the cork from the Zinfandel like she's snapping a bread stick and I'm wondering what this means for the man/wine analogy.

"What about the old 'don't judge a book by its cover' rule?" I ask.

Pulling another bottle from the box, she replies, "In my experience—two out of three—if the label's pretty, the wine is shoddy." Then she whispers, "I usually use the word that rhymes with pretty but I'm trying to be respectful to your mother."

"I don't think she can hear you when she's concentrating on getting her lingerie into the gentle cycle," I say.

"Still, I don't want to get yelled at," she says, moving on to another bottle, whipping the top off in a flourish.

Mom's been married to Dad for twenty-six years and as far as I know, only drinks French Bordeaux, mostly red. Occasionally she can be tempted to try something else. She's just got her way of doing things and she's content with what she knows. I calm myself with the perhaps mistaken belief that Mom's never faced the choices I have—not with men, not with careers versus children, and certainly not with wine.

"This," says Aunt Shirley with reverence, "is a Pomerol. Your mother's favorite. I'll explain later."

"Looks expensive," I say.

"Very. And it's thirty years old in wine years—maybe sixty in human. Perhaps too old for you but we'll see."

"I get it," I say confidently, thinking I'm seeing a pattern. "You've brought wines I'll never be able to find or afford, which is a lesson to, what . . . find a rich man? Never get married?"

Aunt Shirley smiles. "Well, I am the pinup girl for aiming high."

"I'm fine with aiming high," I respond. "I like to aim high, but the targets are all hanging about here." I hold up my hand and, looking beyond it, notice the compost pile my father has been cultivating outside near the back fence.

"Let's keep our metaphors clear," she says, putting another bottle of wine on the table. "This is a Sauvignon Blanc from New Zealand. I tend to think white wines, and the men who love them, are more in touch with their feminine side. That's not a judgment on quality, that's just my opinion. If you like a man who's sensitive, you might look for a man who likes whites."

"Right now most of the men I can think of still drink beer, but then again, that could just be a result of the limited universe in which I've been traveling."

"That," she says, pulling out another bottle, "is an entirely different lesson for an entirely different day."

"What's Bandol?" I ask, looking at the bottle of dark elixir in her hands as she pops the cork.

"Lovely Rhône blend, darling."

"I like blends," I say. "At least in people and animals. I like mutts."

She stares at me, considering whether she should continue if I'm going to say things like this.

"We are trying to move beyond keg parties and cockapoos," she says without a smile. *Just do it, just don't do it.* I guessed it was time to start taking notes.

"Shall we?" Aunt Shirley asks, gesturing at the bottles of wine, open and waiting for us. This is a lesson. I quickly write, "Good men wait." When I look up, Aunt Shirley is pouring champagne into our glasses.

"Yum, I love champagne!"

"Sparkling wine," she corrects me. "From Spain. Champagne is only from one teeny-tiny region in France, unlike my manicure which no decent French woman would ever do to her nails."

She holds her glass up. "To you and your real-world education."

She drinks it down while I begin to sip uneasily, wondering if I should be toasting my success just yet.

"Is this sparkling wine supposed to be like a man?" I ask.

"Actually, it's not part of the lesson, I just knew we'd have something to celebrate. But that said, I do like my men to snap, crackle, and pop, don't you?"

Despite her dramatic delivery of just about everything, Aunt Shirley was never much of an actress. The furthest she got was a walk-on in a Russ Meyer film. She told me one day, after my breasts started to grow (but then stopped before they actually became breasts), that Mr. Meyer said her mammaries weren't large enough for a starring role. It must have cut her to the core because she soon got out of show business and into luxury car sales, where she used her talents to make a killing giving prospective buyers (particularly men) the sense of power and sex appeal that driving a big expensive car can give.

"Here's to all that," I agree, holding up my glass.

"The bowl in the middle of the table is to pour out what you don't drink. If you buy wine you don't like, don't be afraid to dump it down the drain. No sense holding onto a bad investment. Remember the Squasher—and don't doubt for a minute—things *can* get worse."

"I should know that by now," I say. "But I'm writing it down anyway. It's a lesson I find difficult to fully absorb."

"By all means," she says, and with that, she takes my glass and dumps the sparking wine into the bowl like so much dishwater.

"Now, when you're tasting a number of wines, you usually change glasses in between. However, in between men, you only wash. We're family. We'll just rinse."

This I choose not to write, but Mom picks this moment to come back into the room. "I don't know if I like what I'm hearing, but," she says, holding out a glass, "I just came for some wine."

"I'm sorry to say we have not yet poured the Pomerol, but we were about to have a lovely white from New Zealand." Aunt Shirley pours the two of us a glass of Sauvignon Blanc and I see it catch the light of the fading autumn sky outside our house.

"New Zealand!" my mother says as if it's the most exotic, bizarre place on earth.

Aunt Shirley turns to me as my mother scans the wine bottles. "Your mother never ventures far from her favorite wine or your father, but then I suppose if you're married to the equivalent of a Grand Cru, why would you settle for anything less?" It was no secret that my dad was a great guy and that Aunt Shirley envied her sister's long, happy marriage, but it was equally true that they would have been miserable if they'd swapped places. Shirley and Mom share a look that I would sum up as: two roads diverged in a wood—they went different ways but still had the same landscaping.

"I'll have the Pétrus," Mom says.

"Notice she goes right for the French Bordeaux," says Aunt Shirley, pouring the Pomerol into Mom's glass.

"Why all the names for the same bottle of wine?" I ask, slightly embarrassed.

"It's a specificity thing—Château Pétrus is a subset of Pomerol, which is a subset of French Bordeaux, which means wine from the Bordeaux region of France.

"By the way," she says. "I like men from Bordeaux, the Languedoc, Burgundy—"

My mother interrupts. "What kind of men don't you like, Shirley?"

"Men from California?" I suggest.

Aunt Shirley shushes me, then turns to my mother. "You know, you could sit down here and taste something new. It wouldn't hurt."

"But how would it help?" asks Mom. "I already know what I like."

"This is good, Mom," I insist, taking another sip of the Sauvignon Blanc.

But Mom is content. She's practically chewing on her Pétrus as she heads back to the laundry room. When it comes to washing her lingerie, my mother is extremely vigilant. "Keep that red wine away from the camisoles," I call after her.

Aunt Shirley is all business. "There's no point in worrying about lingerie if you don't have a man who appreciates the effort it takes to keep it looking good."

I write that down, assuming I'll figure it out later.

"So here we are, our first still wine," she says, holding her glass up to the light walls of our living room. "Just like your date standing on your doorstep—there's anticipation and examination. Take it all in. Trust your senses but don't rush to judgment. If a wine, or man, doesn't look right, or smell right, it, he, probably isn't right. Don't invite him in and don't even cook with him—you never want to cook with a wine you wouldn't drink."

"But I like this," I repeat. "It's good. I'd go on a date with this wine."

"Dating is fine," she says. "But you're looking for something, someone that makes your body and mind shudder. Wine and men are both 'of the earth' and there are aspects of both that will make you feel organically connected to them when they are 'right.' Don't settle for 'fine.'"

She takes a sip of the Sauvignon Blanc and swirls it around in her mouth. "Crisp, touch of fresh grasses, high alcohol content. Very clean," she proclaims.

"So this wine is, what—the equivalent of a recently showered man from the country who drinks too much?"

"I'd go to lunch with it."

"But not dinner?"

She shakes her head. "But that's just me. You might invite him in," she says.

"Think about it like this, each type of food has a wine that's better suited to it than others. In your parents' case, they're steak and Château Pétrus. Other wines might work as well in someone else's opinion, but to each other, they are a perfect pairing. If you think of yourself as a type of food, what wine goes with you?"

"I'm pretty sure I'm some kind of meat," I say. "Men circle, take a bite, and leave me maimed for the next shark to take a bite. Fortunately, I've always made it to shore to grow back the missing limb."

Now Aunt Shirley rolls her eyes at me, exactly like Mom, her perfect bob swinging perkily around her head.

"In general, the more unique the food—man or woman—the more limited the choices of wine. So for purposes of tasting, we're going to have simple crackers and cheese that will go with all the wines."

"I don't understand how simple crackers and cheese work with the whole 'good man/good wine' thing," I say, trying to stay focused.

"Imagine you're this plate of cheese," she says.

"Hopefully not so plain and chunky looking," I blurt out, a little hurt.

"You're *versatile*," she says. "You need something, some*one* versatile. And even though being versatile is good, it can make it more difficult to find the perfect compliment instead of one that is just okay. Now, if you were a plate of spicy Thai noodles you might want a sweet wine like this Riesling." She picks up one of the bottles and pours us both a glass of late harvest Riesling.

I take a sip.

"I love candy but it makes my teeth hurt after a while."

"Exactly. Do you really want something this sweet all the time?" she asks.

I think about that for a minute. "No. But it would sure be nice to at least try a guy like that."

"Yes," she says, almost reminiscing. "But sweet wines can get insipid and patronizing after a while."

We rinse our glasses, then Aunt Shirley pours the Zinfandel with the flashy label. I hold it up to the light. It's dark but clear, no cloudy particles floating around that might be the equivalent of a guy with pinkeye. I take a big sniff and I swear I can smell cherries and something that reminds me of being outside in the woods as a little girl. It's a good smell. I eat a piece of cheese and get ready to taste. Aunt Shirley is watching me and nodding. I take a sip and it's a whole new world. It turned itself around. And it's all there in the taste.

"Well?" she asks.

"The Sauvignon Blanc didn't have a lot of aroma, but it was good with the cheese. The Riesling was tasty, but it turned the cheese into something less good. But this Zinfandel makes the cheese taste even better. Together they're better than each one alone."

"Sounds like the perfect relationship," says Aunt Shirley. "You're getting it."

"Yeah, those other wines would be like dating a guy who only speaks Inuit. The nodding and small talk is okay, but you can tell from the first minute that anything deeper is not going to work. With this one, the possibilities just opened up."

Aunt Shirley is pleased with me.

"I admit it might take longer to figure this sort of thing out with a flesh-and-blood man, but you can see, there are many similarities. And I was wrong about the label—perhaps even about men from California."

I savor the last of my Zinfandel, sorry to say good-bye. But Aunt Shirley is ready with the next one.

"As I was saying, there are Rhône blends and there are *Rhône blends*. Bandol is not just any Rhône blend." And with that she assumes a pose, lifting her skirt and licking her lips like a prostitute in a Toulouse-Lautrec painting.

"All right, I get it," I say. "I'm not picky enough. I'll work on it."

"This wine is seven years old. That's about forty in human years—a good age for you. Most wines need a little age on them just like a man needs a few life lessons to appreciate a good woman. Some wines, like Beaujolais Nouveau, are meant to drink young. But with the others, if you want 'em young, be prepared for the downside. They can be exciting, but those youthful tannins can bite!"

I'm not sure what tannins are, but I equate them with the shark I mentioned earlier.

I take a sip of the Bandol. Aunt Shirley is watching.

"This is better than the Zinfandel," I say, completely amazed. "It's really earthy and warm but also . . ." I take another sip. "Exciting . . . and it stays there on your tongue, sort of lingering."

"Sexy," says my aunt, and I blush. She takes the glass from my hand and pours out the rest of it, which is a good thing because I don't want to let my getting drunk keep me from learning something important. I realize I haven't taken a note in half an hour and it doesn't seem to matter.

"Now for the Pomerol, Château Pétrus 1972," she says with great deference.

She pours the wine into my glass and I examine it. It's not as red as the others, but still a nice color. It's not as clear either, but then it's been in a bottle for thirty years. It smells older, too, but still good, just older.

"When is old too old and young too young?" I ask.

"Whenever *you* think it is. Sometimes older guys can grow on you. Especially with the kind of reputation and power this wine has. There isn't the bang of the young ones, but there may be something more satisfying. They may also need a little time to open up, particularly to a younger woman. Of course, all wines have a point beyond which they're undrinkable, and that's where a good man is always better than a bottle of wine. A good man is going to be a companion even after he's lost his fruit."

"Shirley, I thought you were going to keep the language clean," Mom says, back on cue for more wine, underwear dealt with. Then she turns to me. "What have you learned, sweetheart?"

"Well," I say, glancing at my unreadable scrawl, "a good wine, or man, has good color, a nice smell, great flavor, when we get around to kissing, and an aftertaste that leaves you wanting more."

I glance up. Aunt Shirley is nodding and Mom is not put off with the sexual references, so I go on.

"He, or the wine, might be young or old. He could be red or white. I have to find the one that goes with the food, or me. I want him open and available with enough complexity to be interesting. A little sweetness is all right, but he can't be saccharine. If I meet him in an exciting place, the real test is when I bring him home. And a man from California could actually be okay. Mostly I just need to use my senses so I can tell when my very own fine wine is right there, sitting opposite me at dinner."

Aunt Shirley is so pleased with her student, she pours out the remaining Pétrus for the three of us. We toast to ourselves as the sun tucks itself behind the trees outside the house. I do not tell my aunt that I'm not sure if I am any more edified about how to meet the perfect guy, but I *am* positive I will avoid the bad ones. And maybe . . . if I only buy good wine . . . a good man just might show up to help me drink it.

The Kitchen Wink

Diana Farrell Serbe

The kitchen wink was not an ordinary wink. No indiscriminate flutter of the eyelid, the kitchen wink was a sign of love, though it emerged from the rivalry between two beautiful sisters. The wink had no rules, no definition, and it never left the kitchen, but it grew to be a symbol of forgiveness, acceptance, complicity, even a rite of passage.

My mother and my aunt were the rival sisters who originated the kitchen wink, though neither remembers who was the first winker, who the winkee. Daughters of an Irish policeman and a woman who died in childbirth, they were catapulted into the kitchen while not yet in their teens. Both became equally adept at roasting a chicken or simmering an Irish stew, though each secretly felt their cooking skills superior to the other's. They managed this competition by ignoring it, but as they matured into their teens a more perilous rivalry emerged: both sisters grew to be quite beautiful, and beauty meant they were attractive to boys. My mother had auburn hair and green eyes; my aunt had flaxen hair and eyes of a brilliant turquoise. Competing for male attention, they polished sibling rivalry until it had a sheen more lustrous than silver. They never acknowledged their rivalry, not in words, and their jealousies went into hiding where they boiled and seethed, waiting for expression.

The sisters were also different in temperament, which showed up most dramatically in their different approaches to cooking. My mother was restrained, my aunt tempestuous. When my mother cooked, she was orderly. She would proceed efficiently, dirtying a minimum of kitchen equipment, cleaning as she went along. My aunt, on the other hand, prepared nothing. She called on help from every pot and pan, every spoon, knife, and fork, all of which would fly from counter to counter whether used or unused. She never cleaned as she went, and her kitchen was battle-scarred by the time the meal was ready.

Knowing his daughters well, their father suggested they cook on alternate nights. The sisters insisted that no, no, no, they loved the camaraderie of cooking together. Entering the kitchen, they would smile at each other, but as soon as they had tied on their aprons, the gleaming perfection of their rivalry lit the kitchen. As the meal progressed, high-pitched sounds of vocal distress rang through the whole house. With turquoise eyes flashing, my aunt would decree, "You cut those potatoes too big. They're way bigger than the carrots." Tossing her auburn hair, my mother would answer, "They'll get mushy if I cut them smaller. Do you want mushy potatoes in the stew?" "Mushy potatoes? Are you calling my potatoes mushy?" Pots and pans unwittingly entered the fray as the sisters banged and tossed them in dramatic expressions of disapproval. Footsteps grew heavy and fast. The unspoken rivalries emerged from hiding: this was war.

I was witness to their battles when only six months old. The oldest child in a family that would grow to four, I was brought into the kitchen and seated in a high chair. No adult family member risked entering the kitchen, but for me escape was impossible. I did the only logical thing a trapped child could do—I joined the drama, cheering on the competing sisters with noisy slaps on the high chair tray and delighted shrieks that transcended their already stentorian shouts. This was drama, and a unique one that no theater could rival, for when the drama swelled to a crescendo, intoxicating aromas rose into the air, and the heat of cooking permeated the room, wrapping us in softness. And then the magic happened. When the food was ready, right there in the midst of the war-torn kitchen, my mother and her sister would look at each other and wink. Having witnessed the battle from my high-chair perch, I also witnessed the truce.

Even at six months, I knew this wink had something to do with love. I wanted to be part of that love and tried to wink, an effort that resulted in fluttering lashes and a wriggling nose, a face that made my mother and aunt burst into laughter. Then they'd both turn and wink at me, holding tight to the wink so I would know that I was part of kitchen life. The wink was more comforting than a blue blanket.

When my mother and I were alone, I would slap my hand on the high chair to elicit a wink. Tray-slapping was highly successful, and the wink became a ritual. As the years passed, and I grew from baby to toddler to little girl, the wink was accompanied by chocolate-covered spoons or bowls that needed to be licked clean. When the number of young children in the family went from one to four, my mother had less time for cooking, and the wink changed to a quick twitch. It was a shorthand wink, but I knew its significance.

The wink took on a more profound significance when I reached nine and experienced my first adult emotion, that of loss. My best friend announced that her family was moving. I was inconsolable. Noticing my sadness, my mother invited me to the kitchen to chat while she cubed meat for the Irish stew that she made especially to comfort me. I was not to be comforted, however, for this was tragedy of Greek proportions. I watched my mother without interest, hardly caring if she winked or not. My mother noticed my listlessness. After a few days, she came to me and said she wanted to make banana bread, but she was having such a busy, busy day that she needed help. "Could you be my assistant?" she asked, her head tipped to the side as if she were sad to be alone. "You're a big girl now," she urged. "Not little like your sisters. Wouldn't you help me separate the eggs?"

I knew that the separation of white from yolk was a job that only the most adult and sophisticated person could attempt. And now my mother was including me in this activity. Worried that I couldn't rise to the challenge, I didn't answer.

"I need you," she added. Experiencing my own loss, I knew what it was like to need a friend and nodded yes with extreme gravity. I had to try to help my mother, even if I failed.

She brought out more eggs than the recipe required. To guide me, she demonstrated the correct method of egg cracking, then went on to the precarious job of separating, continuing to give instructions as she went. "Now, once the shell is broken, you rock the inside back and forth, and the white will gradually separate from the yolk." I watched in amazement as the gooey white plopped into a bowl, leaving the golden center round and shining in its eggshell home. My mother was a magician.

One or two of my eggs met with an unfortunate fate when yolk ran into white, but my mother did not criticize. Patient and unconcerned, she watched until I cradled my egg shells more dexterously and finally separated an egg. I looked up at her, smiling in triumph. She reached to my face and rubbed my cheek. "See that. See what a big girl you are. So capable." And then she winked, a very slow and deliberate wink, a never-before-seen, face-scrunching wink that shoved the pad of her cheek up to her eye.

This was the happiest day of my life. Unable to contain myself, I ran to the backyard and spun around a small fruit tree, round and round, my spins less dizzying than the wink. I was a big girl, capable of separating an egg. Not like my younger brother and sisters, I had been accepted as an adult. And when I stopped spinning, I had learned something—that human life had sad moments, but people didn't stop living. There would always be another egg to separate.

Success and a fervid desire for winks of approval propelled me into the kitchen. When my mother deemed me an adroit egg separator, she brought me into the mysteries of creaming butter and sugar, where I discovered that food spoke, not only to the sense of smell, but to other senses. Though butter could be quite demanding, refusing to cooperate if not at the right temperature, when properly softened it blended with sugar in rippling patterns that changed according to the dictates of the creamer. No school crayon or pile of clay offered the artistic possibilities inherent in butter and sugar. I poked a finger in to taste the combined flavors, then rubbed it between my fingers and discovered that sweetness had a feeling, not just a taste.

Soon I became a kitchen regular, my mother's personal sous-chef, an egg separator of all trades, a whisker, a beater, in time even a chopper. Together we produced the simple but hearty fare that the family loved, and my mother taught me subtle kitchen techniques—the light touch needed to shape a meatball so it wouldn't be heavy, the large cut of potatoes bound for a stew, larger than the carrots or they would get soft. "We don't want mushy potatoes in the stew, do we?" she asked. When I laughed and shouted, "No-o-o," her wink possessed an edge of triumph that I didn't understand.

I was quick to learn that the wink was nuanced, conveying a subtle message that belonged to me alone. My younger sisters received winks, but they were merely baby winks, tossed freely and quickly. When I was at my mother's side, however, the wink indicated that I had earned acceptance in the inner circle. I was a kitchen conspirator, one creating the meal that guaranteed smiles at the dinner table, that ensured my younger siblings would sit quietly because they liked what they were eating.

Though one among four equally loved children, I felt special to be her primary assistant, and was even possessive of my position. I floated in this warm cocoon until Thanksgiving arrived. The family celebration would be held at our house and the kitchen would be crowded with other family members. Jealously wanting this attention for myself alone, I wondered if I would get even a shorthand wink. True, I had been accepted as a grown-up in my mother's kitchen, but my acceptance was only partial. Holidays belonged to mothers—lots of mothers. Children ran to play and fathers appeared at the dining table, but never at the stove.

My parents' generation was the last to believe that cooking was women's work, and this attitude was most obvious at holidays. The women crowded the kitchen strewing casseroles on every counter, pulling out mixing bowls and roasting pans, dirtying every wooden spoon available. The kitchen was woman's world, as mysterious and magical as women themselves. Like alchemists, women mixed liquids, oils, and scented powders, producing pots of bubbling elixirs.

Men never entered the kitchen. Men were straightforward. They went to offices where files were arranged alphabetically, and numbers were written in columns. They could never understand a pinch of this and a dash of that. Instead, the men huddled close together intent on a football game, roaring in loud bursts when grown men successfully knocked down other grown men.

But no football player, however powerful, could compete

with the aroma of roasting turkey and the rumbles of a hungry stomach. As the afternoon wore on, the roars abated. The men turned their eyes toward the kitchen, longing to peek into that aromatic room. Unable to resist the commands of the stomach, my father emboldened to approach the kitchen. It was his house, after all.

His house, but hardly his kitchen. Women swarmed around the stove, dealing with the crisis of timing dishes, of finding space among the many pies to put the turkey so it could rest, of making gravy when every burner was in use. My father saw the chaos and hovered in the door frame, his arms crossed protectively over his chest. "Something smells good," he said, his voice so low it was almost plaintive. He cleared his throat, spoke louder, "How's it going?"

One woman answered, "Almost ready, almost ready." At the same time another added, "Just about there." Then my mother, usually so gentle, grew bold and issued a soft-spoken decree. "Now, out of our way."

When my father withdrew, the women made clucking sounds, shook their heads, sighed, and made comments about "these men." And then the winking began—a torrent of winks, an avalanche. Eyelids fluttered, winks bounced around the kitchen, all of them saying that male ineptitude was to be loved and tolerated, but this was woman's territory. Men did not wink and they did not receive winks. They had their games, their locker rooms, but women had the kitchen where they could bond over the shared instinct to nourish.

The feminist movement and profound economic changes altered these life structures. Territorial boundaries grew fuzzy, gender roles blurred. Women entered the workforce where pinches and dashes yielded to filing systems. Needing to feed hungry families, men donned chef's aprons and opened cookbooks. Clutching spatulas as if they were putty knives, they lurched into the kitchen.

Though their efforts were honest, even valiant, no one who iced a cake with mortar could be rewarded with a full-bodied wink. The wink weakened, fell to disuse, almost became an endangered species. It never disappeared, and a half-wink was bestowed on a select group of apron-clad men. These appropriately attired gentlemen never knew the unique status conferred on them by a moving eyelid.

The wink would languish for a generation. In that time, I married and became the mother of a son, then two years later, a daughter. I sorrowed, knowing that I was raising my children with lackluster winks, not recognizing that I was part of the changing world that had driven the wink underground.

My mother had never brought my brother into the kitchen, but both my son and daughter were raised in the kitchen. As babies, they discovered the melodic potential of banging wooden spoons on shiny pots. As toddlers, they explored the visual, inventing artistic peanut butter and jelly sandwiches. On their own, they discovered that by dropping jelly in blobs they could create a jelly version of a smiley face. They were both prepared for the creative aspects of cooking.

I had married an Italian American, which expanded my knowledge of the kitchen. Pasta sat side by side with my mother's homey Irish stew. The undisputed favorite in my repertoire was tortellini with *Bolognese* sauce. As my children grew, they moved from music and design to become participants in the creation of *Bolognese*. When they were small, I let them break up ground meat with wooden spoons. When they grew older and could safely manipulate knives, I let them help chop. They were so familiar with the sauce that they never asked "what's for dinner?" when they saw the ingredients lined up on the table.

I was proud of this sauce, given to making pronouncements while I cooked, and by the time the children reached puberty they could—and did—finish my sentences for me. "Balance and subtlety are the keys to *Bolognese*," I would begin. "Balance between tomato and meat," my daughter would add. "Subtlety in the use of nutmeg," my son would finish.

Only once did I lose my much-prized subtlety and accidentally doubled the nutmeg. On that occasion, my husband said, "Mmm, I like it," and the children declared the sauce the best ever. Seeing my stricken face, my husband quickly said, "I like the other way best. I do. Really." In defense of my *Bolognese*, I continued to make the sauce with subtlety, but just as the wink was in hiding, so was my children's preference for the taste of nutmeg.

It would not stay in hiding for long. One day they returned home from school, tossed books aside, and looked at the ingredients on the table. "*Bolognese*," they shouted in unison. They looked at each other. Taut smiles broke on both faces, taut because they were hiding a secret. "We'll help."

My son hummed in time to the chop-chop-choppity-chop of the knife, my daughter moved sensuously as she mashed canned tomatoes through her fingers. As they worked, they glanced at each other and smiled those furtive smiles. When all the ingredients were simmering, I stepped forward, grater in hand. As the authority on nutmeg, the guardian of subtlety, this was my job.

I sprinkled a delicate amount of nutmeg into the sauce, stirring well to blend it into the other ingredients. When I finished, I asked if they wanted to taste, but they already had spoons in their hands.

"Needs nutmeg," said my daughter.

"Needs nutmeg," echoed my son.

"It's perfect, and you should not fool with perfection," I said, ready to give an oration about balance and subtlety.

"No offense, Mom," said my son grabbing the grater. "Don't worry, Mom," said my daughter handing him the kernel of nutmeg. The guardian of subtlety was suddenly empty-handed, standing to the side watching a delicate sprinkle become a thunderstorm as the aroma of nutmeg permeated the kitchen.

When the sauce was sodden with spice, they dipped in their spoons. "Perfect," said my daughter. "Perfect," said my son. The taut smiles loosened into wide grins, and they offered me a spoonful of sauce.

I blew gently on the spoon, the aroma of nutmeg infusing my nostrils. As I blew on the spoon, I looked at their faces. They were flush with pride and anticipation. I took a noisy sip of the spoon's contents. My eyes began to water as the taste of nutmeg exploded in my mouth. I looked at the faces again, those faces I loved so much. What was a mother to do when confronted with her children's eager faces and a dangerous overdose of nutmeg? Only one thing could save the situation. I winked.

Out of hiding at last, it was a luscious wink, full-bodied and ripe. Neither gender confusion nor the collapse of territorial boundaries could overwhelm love, and the wink had returned in full glory.

That night, when we sat to eat, the aroma of nutmeg hung over the dinner table like an unmoving cloud. My husband inhaled and looked down at his plate, without reaching for his fork.

My son spoke quickly. "Maybe I put a little too much nutmeg in, but it's pretty good." He turned to me. "Subtlety in the use of nutmeg," he said. As he spoke, he winked. Right there in the dining room, he winked.

My Mother's Kitchen

Stella Mazur Preda

walls whisper untold secrets
tired linoleum painfully scarred
creaking floor boards played ominous tunes,
sinister and creepy
even as morning light tickled
window panes and frolicked with shadows
best of all
that old kitchen floor tilted downhill
several inches
    from one end
        to the other

on cold winter nights
we roller-skated circles

up and down its slopes
worked up an appetite
for mother's old-fashioned
sugar cookies
on hot summer days
hazy stagnant air
hung with the aroma of spices
and simmering sweet fruits
as mother boiled and bottled
homemade jams

Mother was at her best
in that crooked kitchen
where walls whispered
sunlight danced with shadows
and the old floor tilted
                    downhill

Mother + Children = Food and Love

Holly Clegg

Food has consistently remained a focus of my family; it not only provides comfort, but togetherness and laughter within our home. And because of my fervor for cooking, I am to blame for this.

My passion for food and cooking developed at a young age. My mother, Ruth, was an excellent cook, always providing homemade meals and, at times, a fresh batch of cookies, but cooking never turned into a hobby for her as it did for me. She always encouraged my passion, however, and I have a fond memory of my parents allowing me to drive, without a driver's license, to our friends' house to borrow butter, my first time in the car without an adult. I also recall the many hours watching and learning from all my mother's Fort Worth friends in the kitchen. I never begged my mother's close friends, Marji (a gourmet cook), Selma, or Marcia (also exceptional cooks), for attention or toys, but I drove them crazy for any and every family recipe they secretly prepared. From my childhood to the present, the taste was as much a reward in my eyes as the recipe itself. In other words, I love to eat!

My love for food and cooking evolved as I watched my own children, Todd, Courtney, and Haley, embrace my culinary obsession. From a young age my kids never got caught with their hand in a cookie jar; however, licking batter out of a mixing bowl was an issue. I guess I wasn't the typical mother, as I didn't play games with my three children; instead, I enthusiastically included them in baking a batch of homemade cookies.

The role of food in my children's lives became apparent with the birth of Todd, my first child. At this time in my life, I catered for my profession, so my focus was divided between raising my child and cooking. Todd spent more time in the kitchen coloring with his crayons and spurring his culinary curiosity than playing outside with trucks, and I always lugged him to the grocery store. His perception of an apple was different from any toddler I knew—when he saw one, he'd say "swan," as he was enamored watching me create apple swans as garnishes in the kitchen. And turnips and radishes magically turned into flowers in his mind.

Child number two, Courtney, loved the spotlight and food from a young age. With Courtney came my second cookbook, a children's cookbook. I love to cook and I didn't want to sacrifice my career, so I did what any resourceful mother would do: I combined them. I thought as a fun promotional idea for a local TV show, I would incorporate my children into my TV segment. In my kitchen, the morning before the segment, my six-year-old son confidently explained to my three-year-old daughter how to "properly" stuff peanut butter into bugles to make stuffed horns. Once the cameras were rolling, however, all Todd could do was stare blankly at the camera, hyperventilating, while Courtney, smiling the entire time, stuck her fingers back and forth into the jar of peanut butter. I tried to keep the segment together with a straight face. At this time, I realized that Todd's role would be limited to my taste-testing guinea pig and Courtney would become my TV accomplice.

When my third child, Haley, was born, my catering era came to an end. With three kids and my husband, Mike, on board, cooking now became even more of a way of life for my family. In the early '90s, with the advent of healthy eating, I started testing healthy, easy, everyday thirty-minute recipes, creating the first book of my *Trim & Terrific* series, and thus beginning my national career.

My career continued to blossom during Haley's younger years and she was the one child who saw me as a successful cookbook author and as a mom, giving me career credit. I vividly remember the time Haley begged me for a piece of a hot Bundt cake coming out of the oven for an intended media trip to Columbia, South Carolina. After cutting her a piece of the cake, she devoured it and said, "Mom, what are you going to tell people when they see a slice missing?" I responded with, "My daughter wanted a piece of cake, so I cut her one." She said, "Wait, Mom, can't you say, my daughter, HALEY, wanted a piece of cake, so I can be famous like you?" With a smile on her face and always ready to eat, Haley qualified as my cooking sidekick from an early age.

As my traveling schedule expanded, I found interesting ways to include my kids beyond just the local level. Courtney, with her American doll in hand, left Baton Rouge and headed to New York with me for a NBC *Today* show appearance. The lights, glitz, and glimmer along with the attention from Al Roker and Ann Curry made a lasting impression on her; she later returned for a *Today* show college internship. Haley also made a New York trip; however, her real debut was on my segment cooking on the Discovery Channel's *Home Matters* program. Even today, my daughters make the treks from wherever they may be to appear on shows or just hang out on the sets, always knowing there is a good meal at the end of the day. Todd continues his role as a taste tester and relies on my New York visits for his fine-dining experiences.

Though my career kept me traveling when my kids were growing up, at home life was always centered around my kids and their friends—everyone knew a refrigerator packed with an array of food and homemade baked goods graced our house at all times. Many of my kids' friends ate their first artichoke, took their first bite of trifle, or experienced a culinary adventure popping into my home.

Even when juggling my kids and career, feeding my family healthy food constantly remained my top priority. Fast food never entered our world as an option. I cooked healthy meals, creating a healthier lifestyle for my family, without anyone even noticing the difference. The kids vividly remember times they asked for a hamburger; I would say, "Okay, I will make you one," and I'd stop at the local grocery for ground meat. No one can believe my girls, still today, have not eaten a McDonald's burger.

As the kids grew older, cooking truly became even more a part of life in our home, from entertaining to volunteerism. Courtney developed and taught a cooking/manners class to disadvantaged children. In Haley's teenage years, she continued the cooking school tradition, offering classes to disadvantaged children as well as children with disabilities. Haley also baked for a hospice, and made birthday and get-well cakes for every occasion. We were able to transfer our passion to help others.

The kids also used cooking as a stress reliever, heading to the kitchen to take their minds off their typical teenage traumas. Even though both girls entered high school at different times, the kitchen became a safe haven for each of them. Whether cooking relieved their stress, or their teachers and friends requested them to bring treats, their reputation was based on their excellent academics *and* their cooking skills. Of course, Todd quickly volunteered for me to bring food for any athletic event or invited his sports team over to our home for a victory celebration meal, which was always my pleasure.

Food has been and continues to be a love of our lives. My children's appreciation for food is not something taught or learned but part of an environment created in our home that I know will transcend to their own homes and families some day. Wherever my daughter Courtney lives, whether it's her Italian semester abroad or an internship in a new city, I e-mail her recipes or give menu advice. Todd, who lives in New York and works long hours as an associate at a private equity firm, has a small kitchen yet still understands the comfort of home cooking. When he has time, he cooks some of his old standbys: Hamburger Dip or a quick chicken favorite. I have one year left at home with Haley and she has really made a culinary imprint on our kitchen. There are times I have come home from traveling to find dinner prepared or a warm cake welcoming my return. The comfort and love I extended to others through food has permanently influenced my children and provided me with such gratification. But best of all, the food we prepare promotes a healthy way of life and keeps us together longer!

Here are a few of my children's family favorites.

HAMBURGER DIP

This five-ingredient, hearty, and satisfying dip is a perfect snack while watching television sports. Serve with chips.

> *1 pound ground sirloin*
>
> *1 onion, chopped*
>
> *½ pound mushrooms, sliced*
>
> *1 (16-ounce) jar salsa*
>
> *1 (8-ounce) package reduced-fat Monterey Jack*
>
> *cheese, cut in chunks*

Coat a heavy pot with nonstick cooking spray and cook the sirloin, onion, and mushrooms over medium heat for 5 to 7 minutes, until the meat is well browned. Drain off excess liquid. Add the salsa and cheese, stirring over medium heat until the cheese is melted.

Makes 20 (¼-cup) servings.

CHINESE CHICKEN AND BROCCOLI STIR-FRY

Two family favorites, chicken and broccoli, are stir-fried for a tasty Chinese meal. Serve over rice.

> 2 pounds skinless, boneless chicken, cut into strips
>
> 1 tablespoon cornstarch
>
> 1/2 teaspoon ground ginger
>
> 1 teaspoon crushed red pepper flakes
>
> Salt and pepper to taste
>
> 3 tablespoons olive oil
>
> 1 bunch broccoli, florets only
>
> 1 tablespoon minced garlic
>
> 3 tablespoons low-sodium soy sauce
>
> 1/4 cup sherry
>
> 1 teaspoon sugar
>
> 1 bunch green onions (scallions), cut in
>   2-inch slices
>
> 1 red bell pepper, seeded and cut into strips

In a bowl, toss the chicken strips with the cornstarch, ginger, red pepper flakes, and salt and pepper. In a large skillet, heat the olive oil and add the chicken, broccoli, garlic, soy sauce, sherry, and sugar, stirring and cooking over a high heat, about 7 minutes. Add the green onions and red pepper, and continue cooking and stirring for another 10 minutes or until the chicken is done.

Serves 4 to 6.

OOEY GOOEY SQUARES

This is my daughter's most requested recipe. She whips these up for school friends and parties all the time.

> 1 (18.25-ounce) box yellow cake mix
>
> ½ cup margarine, melted
>
> 1 large egg
>
> 1 tablespoon water
>
> 1 (8-ounce) package fat-free or reduced-fat
>   cream cheese
>
> 1 (16-ounce) box confectioners' sugar
>
> 2 large egg whites
>
> 1 teaspoon vanilla extract
>
> 1 cup semisweet chocolate chips

Preheat oven to 350°F. In mixing bowl, beat together the cake mix, margarine, egg, and water until well mixed. Spread the batter into the bottom of a 13 × 9 × 2-inch baking pan coated with non-stick cooking spray. In a mixing bowl, beat together the cream cheese, confectioners' sugar, egg whites, and vanilla. Stir in the chocolate chips. Pour this mixture over the batter in the pan. Bake for 40 to 50 minutes or until the top is golden brown.

> *Makes 48 squares.*

My Old Kentucky Home

Cliff Lowe

Summer days in Kentucky can be quite hot and very, very humid. Even the nights can be oppressive. But nature has a way of balancing things, and the hot, humid days are often cooled by summer rain and thunderstorms. There is nothing puny about a Southern thunderstorm, either. It usually begins with the wind lifting as the sky grows ominously dark. Huge, ebony clouds begin to pace across the sky, grumbling along the way, as if anxious to move on to somewhere else. In their restlessness, they seemingly grow angry and hurl huge, fiery flashes of pure heat and energy in the form of lightning bolts able to split a three-foot-thick tree as easily as if it were a matchstick. These storms not only cool the hot summer nights but provide water, in the form of rain combined with nitrogen produced by the lightning, causing plants to grow. This combination of warm days and rain makes wild blackberries grow and proliferate throughout the state.

It is not surprising, then, to find that blackberry cobbler is a cherished Southern dessert. No one made it better than my grandmother. And nobody loved it more than I did. I would probably have fought a tiger for some of my grandma's homemade blackberry cobbler.

She would spend hours and hours in the summer climbing up and down the hills seeking out blackberry patches while enduring hot sun and the thorny canes of the blackberry plant to pick berries to make cobblers for me. She had other grandchildren, but none of them loved Gran's cobblers the way I did; and it became something special between us. She not only endured the thorns of the plant, but also the minuscule biting insects called "chiggers" or "jiggers" (as some of the old folks pronounced it), which would bite the skin and cause a red, itchy bump that irritated for days on end. Sometimes after these excursions, blackberry seekers' legs would be covered with these little red, itchy bumps, and Grandma got her share of them.

But her love and devotion to me would drive her to continue this yearly exercise until she not only had enough berries to make cobblers all summer, she also had enough of them to preserve several quarts of the berries, providing cobblers all winter long. This was fine by me.

Blackberry cobbler wasn't the only distinctly Southern dish my grandma was known for. In the Southern states is a type of cured ham that we simply call country ham (as opposed to "city" ham sold in a deli), and it is one of my favorite things. Some consider it a delicacy. Country ham is made by taking a "green" ham (meaning fresh, uncured, and unprocessed) and rubbing it all over with a cure made of salt, sugar, and "salt petre," also known as potassium nitrate. The hams are hand-rubbed daily with this mixture, and people make sure to work the cure well into the meat and into the end of the bone where the ham was cut. After each rub, the ham is completely covered over with the mix and left to stand in a cool curing room for twenty-four hours; and then the whole process is repeated again. Some folks do this for two or three weeks and some do it for an entire month. At the end of this rubbing period, the hams are then hung in a smokehouse where they are smoked for several hours with a smoke generated by smoldering hickory chips. After that, they are left to hang in a cool, dry area for at least a year to finish curing before eating.

Country hams have a flavor that one generally has to grow up with to appreciate. I have yet to give it to anyone outside of the Southern states area who could appreciate it. It is quite salty and has a unique, pungent flavor all its own. However, because of the curing process, it never goes bad if correctly stored. I once read about an old root cellar that had been buried and forgotten during the Civil War and, upon discovery a century later, was found to contain two or three pre–Civil War country hams. Other than having a somewhat thick dry rind, they were in good shape and still quite edible. The best way to keep a country ham is to hang it in a cool, dry place (we used to hang ours in the basement) and just cut off what you need for each meal. Then cover it with cheesecloth to keep dust off until the next time you need more ham. Nothing makes a better breakfast for yours truly than a couple of slices of country ham accompanied by some homemade biscuits and farm-fresh eggs cooked over easy. Baked country ham is outstanding, too.

My grandmother and I shared a special liking for country ham, and whenever she had any she would always be sure to save some for me. Even when I was a young man in the army and only home a couple of times a year, she would hoard some country ham for me to enjoy when on leave. It was another something special we shared between us: the love of this unique culinary treat.

One day, while stationed at Fort Bliss, Texas, I got a phone call from the Red Cross telling me my grandmother was in the hospital and in serious condition. I came home as quickly as I could, but making arrangements for military leave took a while. By the time I got home, she was in bad shape and so weak she could barely speak. As I stood tearfully by her hospital bed, she waggled her finger at me to indicate she wanted me to bend over close to her. I leaned as near as I could to her face and she kissed me, then whispered in my ear that she had a piece of country ham for me and had hidden it behind some packages in the door of her big upright freezer so the rest of the family wouldn't find it. She instructed me to go immediately to the house, cook it, and eat it so she could know that I got it. To please her, I went to her house, fried up the ham, and ate it. When I returned to the hospital, she had passed away. But she died knowing I got that piece of ham she had so diligently and lovingly saved, and to this day I can't eat country ham without thinking of her.

If you would like to try some country ham or my grandmother's blackberry cobbler, here are the recipes. But I warn you, the cobbler is addictive. Probably not as addictive as my grandmother's cobbler because she added that special ingredient: love. Come to think of it, you can add that special ingredient, too, if you wish, and perhaps someday someone may extol your virtues to the world.

GRAN'S YUMMY BLACKBERRY COBBLER

I cup all-purpose flour

2¼ teaspoons baking powder

¾ cup granulated sugar

¾ cup milk

½ teaspoon salt

¼ cup granulated sugar

2½ cups blackberries with juice*

1. Combine the first five ingredients in a bowl and pour into a 9 × 16 oiled baking dish.

2. Add the ¼ cup granulated sugar to the blackberries and mix well. (Note: If you do not have any juice, add ¼ cup water to the berries.) Heat this mixture on the stove until it boils. Watch carefully to avoid scorching.

3. Pour this carefully over the batter in the baking dish.

4. Bake at 400°F until the top is golden brown.

5. Serve warm, topped with whipped cream or vanilla ice cream.

FRIED COUNTRY HAM

Country ham slices about ¼ inch thick

I tablespoon lard (or cooking oil)

Slices should be thin. Put the lard or oil in a skillet over medium heat until hot. Add slices and cook for I minute, turn over, and cook 1 minute more. Serve hot. (Note: Country ham is already "cooked" from the cure. To cook it any longer will make it tough, dry, and chewy.) If you desire to make "Red Eye" gravy, add ¼ cup water to the skillet, swish it around to mix the drippings, and serve over the meat. Instead of water, my grandmother used hot black coffee to make the gravy.

BAKED COUNTRY HAM

The night before baking, place the ham in a pot large enough to cover it with cold water. Let it soak in this water overnight and until ready to cook, to remove some of the saltiness. Drain and discard the water. Place the ham on a rack in a roasting pan, skin side up. Add enough fresh cold water to cover the bottom of the pan, making sure the water does not come above the rack on which the ham rests. Cover and slow-bake at twenty minutes per pound in a 300-degree oven. When it is done, remove the ham from the pan and let it rest for twenty minutes before carving. Note: This ham does well when baked in an oven roasting bag.

In Popo's Kitchen

Rosemary Gong

Take a pinch of dough the size of a peanut. Roll it into a ball. Place it in the round pastry with the sweet coconut and sesame bits. Fold into a half-moon.

Popo, my grandmother, whispers instructions as she watches my hands. When a grain of sugar escapes my pastry pouch, her voice will raise an octave. I'm determined to be a good study. But the hard part is coming.

Popo tells me to pull and fold. Pull and fold the half-moon pastry's edge into a curled rope. This is the hard part. Use fingertips to press down the edges. Her method is by memory and rote. Popo doesn't read or write. She makes an **X** for her signature. The kitchen is her domain and she commands it with the force of an emperor's sword.

Popo starts every day by putting on a greengrocer's apron and boiling water in her aluminum kettle. She steeps *bo-lay cha*, a dark rich tea of fermented leaves, by rinsing the leaves first and then filling a large red tartan Thermos with hot water. Any remaining water is poured into a thick glass bottle for drinking during the day. We never drank from the tap. She'd set the Thermos of tea and water bottle to the left of the double sink. At the kitchen sink was a huge window that overlooked the grassy yard, a chain-link fence, a Union 76 station, and an A&W burger stand beyond. Popo lives in Patterson, a small town in California's heartland.

Popo never made tea before she married Gung, my grandfather. She came from a rich family and chores were not expected. When Popo was delivered for marriage, a handmaiden accompanied her for household duties. But my grandfather's family in China couldn't afford to feed another mouth, so the maid was sent home. Whatever bitterness Popo swallowed was long ago. Today in America Popo says everybody works.

Popo hands me more half-moons to pull and fold. The half-moons are called *gok jai*, a Chinese New Year cookie that contains a pocket of sugary coconut, roasted peanuts, and sesame seeds. She takes the cookie sheet of half-moons and walks over to her frying wok and tests the deep oil by dropping in a piece of dough. When the crust bubbles, the oil is ready.

Popo's kitchen is in the back of a family grocery store. Two large carbon steel woks are the focal point. They sit center stage when entering the kitchen from the stockroom. Popo's woks are built-in and the gas flames shoot up from underneath. She regulates the heat by the small ivory-colored knobs below. The wok on the right glints like onyx. It's used for cooking with oil. The wok on the left is dull, dark steel with a water ring around the inside. It's for steaming and boiling. There is a long water faucet from the back wall that swings between the two woks so Popo can effortlessly clean her woks with a few swishes of water and her bamboo brush.

Popo clears the table of cookie ingredients and lays a wet towel over the jewel-edged *gok jais* for safekeeping until after lunch. I walk over to the cement washbasin in the kitchen's far corner to wash my hands. The basin is deep and intended for serious cleaning such as soaking massive quantities of garden vegetables, gutting fish, rinsing swimsuits, and occasionally for cleaning dirty cloth diapers. Popo's washboard sits up against the inside basin—for emergencies—even though she has a Maytag washer sitting to the right. If the Maytag repairman only knew.

"What's for lunch?" says Sherli, my teenaged auntie whose fifteen years is closer to my age than my mom's. Sherli is more like my big sister and I admire her independent streak. When Sherli was younger, she'd plop herself in a red chair against the side of the refrigerator and we'd watch the black-and-white

TV for hours while everyone worked in the grocery store. To-day, she sneaks out to a neighbor's house. When it's time to eat, Sherli magically reappears. Soon, she'll be put to work in the store stocking shelves, boxing groceries, and ultimately, collecting money—that is—if she can be found.

"*Tung-no fun*," replies my grandmother. This is Popo's ver-sion of mac and cheese. It's a far cry from Kraft. Popo pulls out two rectangular Pyrex casserole dishes from her O'Keefe and Merritt oven containing large tender elbow macaroni swim-ming in a tomato, onion, and ground beef sauce. Slices of melted American cheese ooze on top. My Asian palate hasn't taken a liking to cheese yet, so Sherli uses her fork to wipe the cheese off my plate and it goes directly into her mouth.

"Sherli, go tell everyone lunch is ready," says Popo. My young auntie heads out the kitchen door to the stockroom. Sherli was born "Shirley" but she didn't think the original spelling portrayed her personal style, so she modified it when she was in the seventh grade. It stuck without my grandparents knowing. After all, Sherli still sounded like Shirley.

One by one, in short shifts, Popo feeds the store's workers. Popo's motto is if you work, you eat. My uncle Harry brings along a deliveryman who has timed his drop around the lunch hour. My uncle turns the television station to boxing and Sherli expresses her dissatisfaction by groaning and rolling her eyes. She hates boxing, but Uncle Harry always has his way when he's in the kitchen.

After lunch, everyone cleans up after themselves. Only my grandfather, uncle, and the visiting deliveryman are allowed to leave their dishes unwashed in the sink. As the deliveryman leaves he rubs his belt buckle and says, "Thank you, mama san! See you next week."

"Okay!" Popo enthusiastically replies, while muttering under her breath in Chinese that he's got a hungry mouth.

Popo refocuses on the platter of half-moons and asks me if I want to continue pulling and folding by asking, More? As I nod in agreement, I notice Sherli has slipped into a swimming suit she got on sale and has thrown on her winter coat. She's dressed for an outing to the A&W for a root beer float. Popo says, No-go. But Sherli doesn't know no. I heavily weigh the options. I want a root beer float, too, but I'm conflicted by abandoning Popo and our *gok jais*. The idea of going out for a creamy treat with Sherli seductively pulls me. Tailing closely behind her, I head toward the door and fold one step away from being out of sight. In the darkness, I watch my autonomy evaporate. At nine years, I know no.

Popo fries up a batch of half-moons. She turns them in the sizzling oil by using a pair of extra-long chopsticks made just for cooking. Once the cookies turn golden brown she removes them with a wire mesh strainer and lays them on paper towels for cooling. I can't wait to taste one but she says *gok jai* are always better when eaten a day after frying. This allows enough sitting time for the oil to drain from the pastry and become light and flaky—a term she calls *soong*. But I initially hear her say "soon"—and I wonder how tomorrow can be considered soon?

The half-moons are folded tight. They've remained sealed when frying so no sugar particles escape to muddy up the oil. Popo reaches into a tin can hidden on a shelf above the woks that stores salt, sugar, cornstarch, soy sauce, and oil—the five essential ingredients to Chinese cooking. She pulls out a red envelope of lucky money and hands it to me. I say *doh jeh* (thank you) and skip out into the stockroom to find my mom to show her my good fortune. I wonder if it's too late to catch Sherli at the A&W, but the sliding door leading outside is locked, so I'll be going nowhere.

Popo begins the next round, dinner. She removes the lid from a fifty-gallon drum stored next to her stove and measures rice by using a small rice bowl and pours several bowls full into a large pot. She washes the rice in her kitchen sink and lets it soak in the water before cooking. She keeps a few cups of starchy rice water to pour into her wok for cleaning. The starch is a gentle way to help remove the grit from cooking.

While Popo washes *go-gai* leaves, which look like prickly stemmed arugula, she tells me to go into the store for a bunch of cilantro. I walk through the stockroom, which is full of shadows. I peek around corners and behind stacks of cardbord boxes afraid I might see a mouse or a red-spotted black widow. I glance toward my aunties' bedroom doors, the bathroom, and leap through the swinging double doors into a buzz of grocery store activity.

The store is bright with fluorescent light. The meat saw is whirling while Uncle Harry is grounding hamburger. The water hose is sprinkling down the produce case. The cash register ker-chunks while paper bags are snapped open. I want to linger and watch the color of my family's life. But the family kids aren't allowed in the store unattended for long. Uncle Harry calls me over and hands me a package of meat wrapped in pink butcher paper and tells me to take it to Popo. Before doing so, I tiptoe into the candy aisle and nab a few pieces of penny candy for my pocket. I tell myself that Popo won't mind. I pocket another one for her and skip back to the kitchen before she comes to get me.

I'm hoping the pink package holds the contents for my favorite dish—steamed boneless chicken with Chinese sausage, black mushrooms, and flat fungus, which we call elephant ears. But Popo has walked over to the shelf that holds jars of preserved salty lemons, salty eggs, salty greens, and salty fish. She reaches for the lemons and I know tonight's fare will include steamed chicken with preserved lemon.

The package of meat reveals pork spareribs cut in one-inch pieces. This means either soy sauce or black bean sauce spareribs. By the ingredients Popo collects—sugar, salt, and black soy sauce—it's my first guess. She pours, mixes, sprinkles, and then pours some more—using rice bowls, spoons, and pinches from her fingertips as measuring devices.

Watching *gok-jai* cookies cool is a cruel charge for a young girl. Popo can tell by my frequent visits to the platter that tomorrow is not soon enough. She breaks her rule and hands me one, telling me I must have a cup of hot tea with the sweet. As I taste the fruit of my labor, it's flaky, it's sugary, it's satisfying. Popo laughs. My moment of pleasure is also hers.

My working family begins to gather into the kitchen for dinner. My cashier aunties, my butcher uncles, my box-boy cousins, and my grandfather. Sherli too reappears, red cheeked and excited. She runs over to Popo, who is stir-frying fuzzy melon in the wok, and she proudly announces in Chinese, "I got my t-h-i-n-g!" As a sophomore in high school, Sherli is elated and relieved to finally be initiated into womanhood. Popo's face turns sour and she responds with a loud, "SSSShhh! No talk."

Popo's kitchen is not a place to talk about girly things—

things that were once considered shameful—and especially not in mixed company.

Steaming bowls of fluffy rice and a family dinner of *go-gai* soup, soy sauce spareribs, preserved lemon chicken, braised cabbage and bacon, and fuzzy melon with scrambled eggs are on the large, red round Formica table. Dinner conversation is all business—the day's grocery sales, the meat order for a labor camp, the freeloading deliveryman—everything but Sherli's t-h-i-n-g.

Sherli is not eating. She sits with her arms crossed and complains that she hates Chinese food and chopsticks cramp her hand. Popo holds a look of exasperation. I lift my rice bowl and chopsticks higher into my face while peeking over the rim. I watch Popo rise from her chair. She takes Sherli's rice bowl and tosses it into the kitchen sink and then walks over to the refrigerator where the flyswatter sits—this is Popo's last straw. Minutes later, Popo places a small plate of tomatoey macaroni in front of Sherli and hands her a fork. Today, Sherli is victorious. Suddenly my appetite changes, none of the Chinese dishes before me taste good. I want what Sherli has.

Late at night Popo fusses with the family altar. It sits in a quiet corner on a small shelf next to the kitchen door near a cabinet full of medicinal herbs and remedies. The altar holds a bowl of rice to prop up several burnt incense sticks and small cups of tea. On special days Popo places tangerines or an orange on the altar with a red envelope. Tonight she counts her family's blessings.

Whatever was said or unsaid in Popo's kitchen, it was witnessed by two woks, an altar, and a red round table. Outside the big window the world awaited. Uncle Harry found his spot in the Mother Lode country. Sherli settled in a cottage with a collection of furry creatures that would make Dr. Doolittle proud. After feeding and rearing three generations, Popo hung up her green apron for good. The flame under her woks died out. The kitchen was never the same. Popo's kitchen was many things—living room, nursery, way station. It was a place where we came and went. Little did I know that it too would come and go.

Dorry's Blue Crab Bliss

Tina Miller

By the late sixties, single-parent households were not uncommon. For my brother and me it was a bit different because my father got full custody of us.

Like all single parents my father worked a lot to keep a roof over our heads. There was nobody at home hunched over a simmering stew all day. By the time my father got home from a long day, a simple dinner was cooked and we ate together.

In 1976 my father built my grandparents a year-round home in Chilmark. As a girl growing up without a mother present, I became close to my grandmother Dorry Miller.

My grandmother grew up in an educated middle-class family in western Massachusetts. She was the daughter of an eccentric genius of a man named Allan B. Hendricks, also known as Pop. Pop was fourteen when he entered high school, but didn't like it much and left after a few days. For the next few years, he educated himself reading the entire *Encyclopaedia Britannica* and many other books of knowledge. At eighteen, Pop entered Harvard. Pop met Sallie Fox Acken, who was attending Radcliffe. She was a talented musician who had studied in Paris under Paderewski. The couple married in 1908 and had three children. My grandmother was the second child born. After Harvard, Pop went to work for General Electric, where he became known as the Leonardo da Vinci of transformers.

Education was a focus in the Hendricks home and Dorry was encouraged to go to college. She entered Smith College in 1929 with German as her major. After some mix-up with the letter G she ended up with a major in Greek, and that worked out fine for the good-natured Dorry.

With her Lauren Bacall looks and a great education in her pocket, Dorry eventually did what many eligible women did in those days: she met a brilliant handsome man, Richard R. Miller. Richard R. Miller, known as Dick, was in born in Europe. He came to western Massachusetts to attend Williams College after studying at private schools in Paris. Soon after Dick and Dorry were married, Allan, their first-born child and my father, was born in 1942. My grandfather was soon shipped out as a Navy engineer.

After returning from the war, my grandfather resumed his

work as a French professor. My grandmother lived the life of a professor's wife, raising their two sons and working quietly as a secretary at whatever private school Dick Miller taught at.

In the late forties, my grandparents were offered six acres of land on Martha's Vineyard. John Whiting, also a professor and a good friend, offered my grandparents and several other families plots of land in the boondocks of Chilmark. At the time, Dick and Dorry Miller could not necessarily afford it, but they bought the land anyway. The property included a beach lot on the south shore of the island at a place called Quansoo.

Quansoo is located on the Tisbury Great Pond, which hugs the south shore of the island. The Tisbury Great Pond is more lake-sized and filled with brackish water, part salt, part fresh, the home for oysters, soft shell clams, eels, and blue crab. During certain times of the year, a channel is dug from the southern edge of the pond to the ocean and the two waters mix. For kids, it's a mini river rapid between the vast pond and the Atlantic.

The property my grandparents bought was down a two-mile dirt road without electricity or a telephone. They had a small cabin built with a gas hot-water heater, a small gas fridge, and a red hand pump for running water out of the kitchen sink. We called Quansoo "Down Pond."

It was such a great time when my grandparents would come for their summer visit.

Down Pond was cool! We played crazy eights with the dim but warm light of the kerosene lanterns. It was pretty much like camping, but the little cabin was dry and cozy. My grandfather would take us out on his eighteen-foot sailing canoe, exploring the coves of the pond. There were cocktail parties between the five families who shared the rustic life on the pond. It was definitely a magical place for my brother and me.

After my grandfather retired from teaching, my father added a year-round house onto the cabin and my grandparents settled at Down Pond. With the new addition, the house on Down Pond was less rustic and now filled with fine antiques, furniture, and china. Down Pond became very civilized, though they had only recently gotten a telephone, and electricity was a few years away. For now they relied on a windmill and a generator for power.

Several times a month, we would have dinner with my grandparents.

Attending dinners at Down Pond was a bit of an event, with linen on the table, silver settings, Limoges china, silver wine coasters, and a really neat silver butter dish that had a slot to hold ice to keep the butter chilled. I loved the ceremony of it all even though my manners and vocabulary were often challenged.

As far as dinner went, my grandmother had a pretty simple repertoire: really good roasted chicken, baked spaghetti with meat sauce, and baked ham, which always was served with the all-time best macaroni and cheese. As soon as we arrived, I went right to the kitchen and flung open the oven door to see what smelled so good. There was salad served *after* the main course, thanks to my grandfather's European upbringing, and simple desserts like vanilla ice cream with real maple syrup and cookies. At these gatherings, my grandmother usually cooked unless it was steak or lamb; red meat was man's work and my grandfather took care of the "beast," as he called it. He stood over a medium-rare roast sharpening his silver carving knife like he had just made the kill. We always devoured everything on the table. Between my brother, who was almost a foot taller than me, and my dad, there were never any leftovers.

My grandmother and I were quite close, maybe because I was the oldest female grandchild, another woman in a male-dominated family. Grandma and I both loved family history and photographs. We would sit on the brick sun porch and she would pull out old family photo albums. I would pepper her with millions of questions about the family. My grandmother was the link to the family tree. With the memory of an elephant, she introduced me to many family members gone by. Now that she is gone I wished I asked another million questions.

My grandmother was very fair and generous and never

spoke of anyone in a negative manner, unless they done one of her Miller men wrong—then, watch out! She was very loyal. My grandmother loved to read and send cards and letters. From her I learned the importance of a thank-you card.

In the last years of my grandmother's life, she began sharing certain histories not spoken of before. She became downright loose-lipped at times and opened up the vault. She told me about my mother, and what she was like when she was younger. She told me what she thought had split my parents up when I was three. She filled in some gaps in time for me. I treasured this intimacy and trust that we had.

One night after dinner, Grandma revealed that she did not really like to cook. I was stunned. Maybe after all the cooking she had done for so many years, it finally got old, or maybe she truly never enjoyed it, but like a good wife had done her part.

Whether she truly dreaded cooking or just lost interest, I know Grandma did have one true passion with food.

By late July, the Tisbury Great Pond would fill with blue crabs. That time of year I refused to walk in the pond without sneakers on for fear of getting pinched. That same time of year one of the Miller men—my grandfather, father, brother, or uncle—would walk down the grassy path to the pond with an empty bucket and return with a bucket full of Grandma's favorite: blue crab.

At that point, all other activities like laundry and trips to town would be put on hold; she was on a mission. Grandma would steam the crabs, let them come to room temperature, then stand in front of the sink all afternoon picking crabs. By cocktail hour, a bowl of blue crab mixed with Hellmann's mayonnaise and black pepper was presented with a plate of saltine crackers. I paced myself, trying not to be greedy about that fabulous crab salad, knowing the labor of love that my grandmother put into that precious bowl.

I am not sure if I believe my grandmother did not like cooking. How could such delicious tastes and smells come from anywhere but a happy kitchen and cook?

Those dinners were early grooming for me on the pleasures of food and the whole experience of dining, conversation, and family and a never-ending love for the kitchen.

These days, though I still cook almost every night, I admit there is not too much ceremony. Our two boys tend to eat earlier, because they begin begging at five and with all the drama they can muster tell me they are *"starved!"* My husband gets home after five and basically needs to unwind and do stuff with the boys, who have lots of important things planned for his arrival home. As the house quiets down, my husband and I finally sit and eat. I know that as time goes on, we will level out and we can have a bit of that good old-fashioned ceremony, and maybe then the boys can carve the beast.

It has been fourteen years since my grandmother died, and

to this day my record for being on time is indisputable. I am a thank-you card sender, so are my boys. I have assembled twelve photo albums and I love to talk family history with them.

I adored my grandmother, Dorry Miller, and believe she put a positive stamp on me, but one of the things I am proudest of is that she taught me how to make a killer roasted chicken: moist, full of flavor, and falling off the bone.

My Mother-in-law's Kitchen

Harriet Rochlin

At first glance, I was struck by the variegated ambiance of my mother-in-law's kitchen. On the east wall stood a new (1946) electric range, and in the southwest corner, the old stove my mother-in-law favored for baking breads and cakes. Scarred pine drain boards crowded with Mason jars, electrical appliances, and draining dishes flanked the sink. Above, tall windows admitted north light and a view of rounded hills bearded with amber Mexican hay. In the center was an oak table big enough for gallons of peaches and plums cut up for compote; corn husks spread for a hundred tamales; a lug of *ugerkes*, cucumbers, for pickling; or a *koldre*, a feather bed, for a sick child. Near the back door was the pantry where she stored beef and tongue in tall corning crocks with rock-secured lids, tin boxes of homemade sweets, and jars of preserved fruits. In days of less money and greater strength, I was told, my mother-in-law kept chickens, turkeys, a cow, and the pantry reeked of newly laid eggs and curing cheese.

Adjoining the kitchen was the breakfast room with western windows framing a rock-walled desert garden—palo verde, mesquite, ocotillo—a feeder for migrating birds, a hammock stretched between tall junipers, and on the far side of the driveway, a ramada and a native rock barbecue pit. In the background was Ambos Nogales—Arizona and Sonora—wearing a gray-blue veil of mesquite cooking smoke and straggly patches of colored lights at night.

I, a city girl, had read about self-sufficient kitchens in isolated country houses, but never one like my mother-in-law's. Taken one at a time, I could identify the smells, tastes, sights, and sounds as American, Jewish, and Mexican. I grew up in Boyle Heights when the population was predominately Jewish and Mexican, and was a product of the same tri-cultural amalgam. But the blend in my mother-in-law's kitchen was stronger, and closer to the core. Consider the meals my round-faced, bosomed, bellied mother-in-law served three times a day, seven days a week.

Breakfast was American fare—canned fruit juice, eggs, cereal, pancakes, waffles, toast, butter and jam. All were cooked to individual order, speedily and efficiently with the aid of a toaster, percolator, waffle iron, griddle pan, egg timer, blender, mixer. (My father-in-law jokingly complained she had more labor-saving appliances in her kitchen than he had on the shelves of his hardware store.) The breakfast table accommodated six, in a squeeze, eight. You were served, you ate, chatted, or studied the matinal desert and cityscape, and then you were on your way. My mother-in-law and her current assistants, Juana, Rosita, Felicidad, whisked away your plate, eager to complete the breakfast chores and start on the next meal.

Lunch was slower, more substantial, and in the Mexican style, followed by a siesta. My father-in-law returned from town to eat each day, and often brought guests. The fare then and at the family's evening meal most days was a hearty mixture of American and Eastern European Jewish dishes. Each repast had a beginning, middle, and end. For starters there was chopped herring or liver, marinated peppers, or fruit. Next came a freshly made soup—chicken with noodles or matzo balls, mushroom and barley, or split pea—followed by a main course of fowl (some years homegrown), fish, beef, or a Russian Jewish delicacy—cheese blintzes, latkes, knishes, *holiskes* (cabbage rolls). Then came dessert—fruit, strudel, cookies, honey or sponge cake, sometimes coffee, but mostly tea, à la Russe.

Sunday and holiday lunches were served in the dining room on a home-embroidered tablecloth set with china, silver, and crystal. The table extended to seat a seemingly limitless number of guests. According to my mother-in-law, an enthusiastic partygoer, if you want to be invited, you have to invite.

My mother-in-law acquired a taste for Mexican food soon after she settled on the border, and learned to prepare local dishes with minor modifications for her own and, by emulation, her family's tastes. Spicy seasonings she loved; I never heard her complain a dish was too *picante* or *chiloso*. But pork, prized by Mexicans, forbidden to observant Jews, she eschewed, but not for religious reasons. After she left her parents' Orthodox household, her dietary habits were governed by pocketbook and palate. Shellfish and other nonkosher foods she learned to enjoy, but *hazer*, pork, never. So she substituted chicken and easy-to-shred beef for pork, and Fluffo for lard when preparing her enchiladas, tacos, tamales, frijoles, arroz. Most of her children and grandchildren became passionate aficionados of her style of Mexican cooking, and several family members have carried her inventions to new heights. One son tells of a midnight ride on a Nogales-bound bus when he was summoned home from college to visit his mother who was desperately ill with pneumonia. Bouncing along, tears on his cheeks, he guiltily recalls thinking: if Mama dies, who will make the enchiladas?

Marketing for my mother-in-law was both a chore and a social event, especially during the later years. Her husband dead, her children gone, alone in the house except for a house-keeper-companion, she often would go to Puchi's, her favorite market, two or three times a day. She also shopped at the Mexican *mercado* across the line.

Up until a few years ago, the *mercado* was crude and countrified. Hooked quarters of beef, chickens, turkeys, and rabbits hung from the ceiling, and fish, hacked and oozing, lay on gouged wooden blocks. Blood-splattered entrails, fat, and discarded bones were scattered everywhere. Undaunted by the carnage, the swarms of flies, the stench, my mother-in-law plunged in, made her selections, bargained jocularly with *el carnicero*, the butcher, or *el pescadero*, the fish vendor, dumped her newspaper-wrapped purchase into her shopping bag, and left delighted with her bargain, *ganga, metziah*. In the produce section she bought Mexican-grown lettuce, tomatoes, onions, cantaloupes, watermelons, which were plentiful and cheap.

From the *mercado* she'd move on to the *panadería* for *bolillos*, Mexican rolls, and to the *tortillería* for handmade tortillas. If she passed the *ostionero*, the oyster man, she'd stop at his cart and consume on the spot fresh oysters doused with a red cocktail sauce and served in the vendor's only glass. People greeted her on the streets and she responded in serviceable Spanish bearing the markings of English. Which brings to mind my mother-in-law's language(s). She unconsciously slid from one to another, at times using English, Yiddish, and

Spanish in a single sentence. "*Formacht la luz* in the living room." "*Tome* this plate *fun mir*." Adding the suffixes of one language to the roots of another, my mother-in-law created her own words: *kvetchton*, a big hug or squeeze; *besoleh*, a little kiss; *schmecton*, literally, a big smell, figuratively, a look around. She spoke as she moved: rapidly. When someone didn't understand her, she repeated her remarks in Spanish.

With the Sonoran women who worked for her, my mother-in-law was just and straightforward. Having been a seamstress in a sweatshop, she was a sympathetic *patrona*, employer, but everyone worked, and no one longer or harder than she. Able employees earned praise and affection, the distracted, dishonest, or complaining, chastisement. Working side by side, she and her helpers chatted. She knew their origins, vital statistics, and current concerns. Asked or unasked, she offered advice but didn't expect them to alter their ingrained ways. The longstanding ties between her and these women ultimately proved fortuitous. For the last four years of her life, unable to walk, feeble but cheerful, she was cared for consecutively, then jointly, by two sisters, Marta and Consuelo, who saw to her needs as though she were one of them, which, in part, she was.

CHEESE ENCHILADAS

Soon after I married, my young husband started hankering for his Mama's cheese enchiladas, homemade Sonora style but with a Jewish twist, vegetable shortening instead of lard. The next time we visited Nogales, he asked her to teach me the recipe. I went with Mama to buy the ingredients across the border in Nogales, Sonora— a fresh chunk of white Mexican cheese cut from a large wheel, dried chiles—long, dark red ones, short skinny red ones. I wouldn't remember the names but I did recall what they looked like. The tortillas were also from across the line, newly made, warm and pliable. Back in Los Angeles, I could have found comparable ingredients by driving to one of several local barrios, and initially did. As my familial and professional duties mounted, I increasingly resorted to packaged cheeses, eschewing readily available Monterey Jack and straying to extra-sharp cheddars. Rather than starting from scratch with dried chiles, I was soon substituting canned Las Palmas Enchilada Sauce, Hot, for the family, Medium or Mild for company. In 1981, when the *Arizona Jewish Post* invited me to recall my mother-in-law's cooking, I assembled this replica of Mama's made-from-scratch enchiladas.

SAUCE

4 dried chiles Ancho or 4 dried chiles Anaheim
4 dried chiles de Arbol

2 to 3 buds of pressed garlic

1 small yellow onion, chopped fine Jewish style

Salt to taste

1 teaspoon dry oregano, or 1 tablespoon
  chopped fresh oregano

1 piece of toasted bread (to thicken the sauce)

1 ½ cups water

Cut open the chiles and remove the seeds and veins. Soften them in boiling water for three minutes. Pour off the hot water and put the chiles and the rest of the ingredients, including the tap water, in a blender. Blend until smooth. (I strain the mixture through a colander.)

FILLING

1 dozen tortillas—the fresher the better

1 ½ lbs. grated Mexican white cheese—Queso
  Fresco, Panela, or Oaxaca—Cacique, a
  widely manufactured brand, makes all three.

1 small onion, chopped fine

4 tablespoons of pitted and sliced green olives

Vegetable or olive oil

Cover the bottom of one frying pan with oil and heat. Place the enchilada sauce in a second frying pan and heat. Warm both sides of each tortilla in the oil until it is soft. Dip tortilla in the warm enchilada sauce. Remove and place flat on a plate. Spread two table-spoons of cheese over the tortilla, sprinkle chopped onions and sliced olives over the cheese, and roll into a cylinder-like form and place seam down in an oiled baking pan large enough to accommo-date twelve. Pour additional sauce over the top, and sprinkle with cheese. Heat in the oven at 350°F until hot to touch, and serve.

Serves 4 to 6.

Savoring Moments

Lisa Schroeder

While my mother was an amazing cook and had owned a restaurant before I was born, she and I spent very little time together in the kitchen. I can remember her hand-grinding chopped liver for the Passover seder and the smell of simmering chicken soup on the stove, but I was never part of the process, just the beneficiary. For most of my childhood, my mother cooked wonderful homemade meals that we would share around the dinner table. She'd make everything from shish kebab to lobster tails, and the meal was always delicious. My mother had huge themed dinner parties replete with centerpieces and exotic dishes such as coquilles St. Jacques and baked Alaska, and her culinary talents were lauded by all her friends. While she loved to have me at the dinner table savoring her efforts, I was perceived as an annoyance rather than a help in the kitchen, thus shooed away more than welcomed to her side. It wasn't until I was nineteen years old, living in Jerusalem, Israel, that my mother and I finally cooked together, side by side.

I moved to Israel when I was seventeen to go to college, and planned to stay there when I graduated. One month after my arrival, I met Guy, who was born in Morocco, raised in France, and moved to Israel at the same time and for the same reasons as me. We began to live together shortly after we met (an even longer story!), and I tried very hard to be the perfect housewife while simultaneously attending college full-time—assuming all the cooking, cleaning, and laundry duties. Being a snobbish semi-Frenchman, Guy had very particular tastes and a demanding palate, so I spent many hours at the stove trying to cook dishes he might enjoy. Since I was always interested in cooking but knew very little about it, I began to teach myself through cookbooks, desperately wanting, but rarely receiving, Guy's approval for my valiant attempts.

A few months after we began living together, Guy's parents came from Paris to visit us. I immediately saw that the apple didn't fall far from the tree—Guy's father was obsessed with good food and as critical as his son of anything not to his liking. Since I was so eager to please Guy, I begged his mother, Mireille, to show me some of her son's favorite dishes. Fortunately, she happily obliged and provided me with my very first hands-on cooking lessons. I learned mainly through demonstration since our only common language was food—Mireille spoke neither Hebrew nor English, and I spoke very little French. Most of her dishes were Moroccan-Jewish in origin, but she was astute at popular French dishes as well. She showed me how to make such dishes as *poulet au champignons* (chicken thighs browned and braised with garlic and sautéed button mushrooms), *boulettes* with peas (ground beef balls with seasonings, slow-stewed with peas and garlic), and a traditional Sabbath stew, *dafina* (beef short ribs, garlic, potatoes, barley, and eggs in their shell, simmered for nearly twenty-four hours). Invariably, Guy's father would wander into the kitchen and proceed to tell us how the dishes *really* should be prepared, refining what his wife had just shown me, giving additional hints on the expected flavors. Between the two of them, I was learning a cuisine and techniques I knew nothing about. After his parents returned to France, I continued to teach myself to cook, trying new dishes each week, occasionally calling Guy's mother when things didn't turn out quite right or when her son had a hankering for something I had not yet mastered.

After a year together, Guy and I began to plan our wedding. It was evident that our guest list was going to be small, since most of our families were abroad, and besides some close Israeli friends, the only members of my family planning to attend were my mother and father. Because we were still students, we couldn't afford a big wedding, and the monetary wedding gifts our parents promised us had to be used for the wedding itself. We therefore tried to cut corners wherever possible—I rented my wedding dress, the ceremony and celebration were to be at the Hebrew University Synagogue (since we were students there, it was free), and I planned to cook all the food for the event with my mother and mother-in-law-to-be.

Guy's mother flew in a few weeks early and we traveled up to her brother and sister-in-law's house in Kiryat Motzkin, a small town outside of Haifa, in northern Israel, where we spent a week preparing some food and sweets for the wedding. Together, Guy's mother, aunt, other female family members, and I spent four days in the kitchen and dining room, baking, assembling, and plating up cookie trays and homemade condiments for the big event. Once again, the only common language was food, since there was French, Moroccan Arabic, and Hebrew bantered about as we cooked and made up the dishes. At one point, I was assigned to whip the egg whites alone in the kitchen for the meringue kisses, while the other ladies were in the dining room peeling peppers and tomatoes for the *salade cuite* (a slow-cooked tomato and roasted pepper compote). My mother-in-law-to-be would come into the kitchen to check on me, making sure I was whisking the whites fast and long enough. Each time I thought they were stiff enough, Mireille would come back into the kitchen and say, "No, not yet, keep going." She eventually had me place the whites over a bowl of hot water hoping that would help them get even stiffer. I whisked and whisked until she finally gave me the nod indicating we were "there." We stirred in some coconut, piped the kisses into tiny paper cups, and then baked them for what seemed like forever until they were still snowy white but crispy.

The next day, we carefully packed the fruits of our labor into my Volkswagen Beetle and drove the four hours back to Jerusalem to finish the preparations for the wedding. My mother flew in a few days later, just in time to go with me to the mikvah (a ritual public bath the bride takes before marriage to make sure she is "clean" for her husband) and to do the final food preparations. Unbeknownst to me, this was to be the first and last time I would ever cook with my mother. I assigned her just two dishes, which were some of my most favorite—her sweet-and-sour meatballs and roast chicken.

I observed carefully as she seasoned the meatballs with salt, pepper, onion, bread crumbs, and water. I watched her manicured fingernails and translucent hands squeezing, then shaping, the meat into small little balls. Then she gave me her first cooking tip—"Keep a small bowl of cold water nearby for dipping your hands before shaping the meatballs. That way, the meat doesn't stick to your fingers," she told me. I marveled at how long she massaged the ingredients into the meat and then the care with which she rolled each meatball. I was surprised to learn how easy the dish was to make, and the little shortcuts she took in spite of which still yielded one of my most favorite dishes. Cranberry jelly and tomato sauce? That was it? Then she made the roast chicken, seasoning it with just salt, pepper, garlic salt, and paprika. It amazed me how such simple seasonings could yield such tasty chicken. While there was nothing complicated about her dishes, and I had mastered far more intricate dishes such as coq au vin, cooking side by side with my mother in my small Jerusalem apartment kitchen was one of the best experiences in my life. I soaked it all up, relishing how good it felt to be with my mother, one on one. Up until that point, I was a just a child and then an angry teenager who never wanted to listen to my mother. Now, for the first time, I listened to her intently, waiting for the pearls of wisdom to drop from her mouth. It didn't matter how profound her tips or how involved her dishes—it was the first time we ever cooked together, and we were cooking for *my* wedding. My mother had flown thousands of miles to be with me on my special day and helped me prepare for it. My mother was sharing her knowledge and taking the time to show me how to make something she had fed me for years.

The morning of my wedding day, we got up early to set up

the buffet in the covered patio outside the synagogue. I returned home, put on my makeup and rented white wedding dress, and set out for the synagogue. It was around sunset, and the orange sun made all of us glow. My father donned his kepah (skullcap), gave me a good luck kiss, and walked me down the aisle with my mother on the other arm.

I became pregnant a year later and hoped that again my mother and father would flock to my side for the birth of their grandchild. When they informed me they could not travel the thousands of miles back to Israel, I decided I needed to move back to America to raise my child near her family and grandparents. I moved back in early December, my husband followed a couple of weeks later, and my daughter, Stephanie, was born on December twentieth. My mother died suddenly seven months later.

I knew that the time my mother and I cooked in my tiny kitchen in Jerusalem was a special moment. I just didn't know it was going to be the only moment she and I would share in the kitchen, cooking side by side. It was just one of the many times I have been taught the lesson that one must enjoy each moment in one's life. Every experience can be special and delicious, and whether sweet or sour, all must be savored and cherished.

My Mother, My Mentor

Michel Nischan

Your whisper lies in the gentle rub of pea vines against the trellis. Your tender admonishments allow the beetles to play where sufficient care was not taken. The joy of your way fills my heart when I see the wonder on the face of my children as they pull giant carrots from the moist fall soil. And your well-deserved rest is as pure and promising as a fresh blanket of snow over the beds that fed my family and created a season of such wonderment. The garden is the place we meet and I'm glad we're still together. For you, I have only one question: why didn't you tell me about those damned squash borers? No worries, I'll let you know when I figure it out for myself. Thank you for all you have given me. I could not be who I am had it not been for your loving way.

This dedication from my latest book, *Homegrown, Pure and Simple*, is an example of how I privately speak with my mother. She was the maker of me and my siblings, the teacher of all joys, and interpreter of many sorrows—not to mention the cooker of some of the tastiest damned food I've ever eaten. Mom was the one who taught each of us children how to sing, cook, dance, and how to love through each of these valuable expressions (though her favorite medium was food and her kitchen). Though she is gone, her lessons inform me to this day, and her words and ways grow within me each time I turn over a new culinary stone. As I work both here and abroad, I often encounter a new ingredient or technique that profoundly touches me, like *huitlacoche* or applying *sous vide* cooking techniques to fresh ingredients. I sometimes have the privilege to witness amazing historic cooking events, like when I and some of my colleagues cooked for His Holiness the Dalai Lama. I have also been fortunate to witness equally historic cooking events, like a grandmother, mother, and uncle cooking a Kerala Satya in Alappuzha, India—arguing and laughing as they cooked along—only to serve their very best results to the guests they valued more than themselves, as demonstrated by their refusal to eat (just like Mom) until I and the other guests had received the best first portion. When I have these encounters, my first instinct is to go to the phone to call Mom to tell her everything. I catch myself, often with phone in hand, and wish sorely that she were still here.

I have seen many an American chef celebrated for their work in preserving and promoting American cuisine, yet I believe precious few ever successfully present an expression that truly preserves our juvenile and fleeting culinary heritage. I believe American Country Cooking came from family farmers, like my mom and many others in farm communities long past, who knew how to work with the food that grew in their homeland. They knew what to do with the best of the produce, as well as how to use fallen or overripe foods in ways which nurtured the feelings of security and pleasure that only a skillfully prepared home-cooked meal could. I believe our true American culinary heritage was defined during the short period of time when real regional systems of agriculture, fisheries, and animal husbandry were in full force, and the home cooking of many a farmland mother ruled. These systems provided foods that were readily available at peak season, and allowed the birth of dishes from succotash, to pot roast, to Gullah-stewed crabs, to fried chicken, smothered jowls, and collard greens. God gave the whole animal, so the whole animal was to be used. The most difficult cuts yielded the most amazing textures and deepest flavors because of the love, skill, and good intent of the cooking artisans often called Mom. It is difficult to find a celebrated chef, other than Edna Lewis, who simply and completely connected to our true American culinary heritage in this manner.

I have listened to Edna Lewis's words and cooked from her recipes. I believe had Edna and my mom ever met, they would have become fast friends. And had my mom been fortunate enough to have shared her food with others through similar venues to Edna's, she would have been equally celebrated. For few have ever been as passionate and hardheaded when it comes to true home cooking, and to Mom, true home cooking was about more than just the recipe. The best cooking started with the best ingredients, many of which had to be grown at home. Her basic tenets of food and food's relationship to life will never leave me. To me, my mom was one of the last great American country cooks to grace our heritage. I refer to her now as Chef.

Many folks believe their makeup is a result of their many experiences, some intentional and many random, which all blend together with their surrounding environment and relationships to create the being that is their self. I believe my whole life was intentionally directed and planned in a way that ended up equaling me, though I admittedly had little to do with it. There was no happenstance, or at least I like to believe there was not. My mother taught me how to garden and cook because she knew I innately loved it. She always made sure there was a chore for me in the garden and a place for me to work beside her in the kitchen. When I left home to become a musician and was starving, she clipped ads out of the paper to get me a cooking job at a local truck stop. When I resisted her constant prodding, she argued: "The money's good and at least you'll eat. Besides, you're a better cook than a musician." While her frankness stung at the time, there is no debating that her persistence in making me take the job led me to this very day.

If someone had told me ten years ago that one day I would return to the country cooking of my childhood, I wouldn't have believed them. Over the last decade since my son, Chris, was diagnosed with diabetes, I refocused my cooking on health and well-being and was extremely excited about my new direction. So much of the data available led me on a path toward shunning animal fats and, thus, away from my culinary heritage. I thought I would never look back, but that is exactly what has happened. The more I researched, the more studies began to indicate that fat is not the enemy it once was seen as. More indicators are leading toward the happy truth that eating truly fresh and seasonally ripe foods should be at the heart of any diet that promotes good health and longevity. This is what Mom taught us through her gardening and cooking, and I now find myself absorbed by the amazing memories forged at the end of her hoe or from the top of the step stool I used so I could stand beside her and watch the chicken fry.

I am often overwhelmed by the complexity caused by memories of such a simple upbringing. While I find myself constantly turning to and relying on learned standards, I am exposed to a daunting array of new technologies and global food cultures. Reconciling the two is often like trying to pair a young country man who loves fishing, hunting, and watching fireflies over evening fields with a successful young city woman rising to become the first female partner of a well-known law firm. Each life has appeal, while neither could be more different than the other.

Here's how I try to apply many of my mom's teachings to the beliefs that drive my work today:

MOM: Dirt is alive. Without dirt and water, no seed will grow.

ME: Education is the foundation for intellectual advancement. Without education and thoughtfulness, many ideas will not grow and prosper.

MOM: The flavor of a ripe peach is born of the sun and a whole bunch of cutting that might seem cruel to the tree. It's not easy, but the taste is great.

ME : The pain and tribulation of professional advancement for a woman possesses a flavor born of the rights of equality and freedom. It's not easy, but the taste is great.

MOM : The juice that drips from a slice of freshly picked cucumber is rain.

ME : Equality is the lifeblood of freedom.

Interestingly, after all of the lessons I remember and the thought that I vest in them when applying them to the here and now, I find my mother's presence to be most abundant when I am working in the kitchen. Knowing, unconsciously, that Mom was the world's biggest proponent of not complicating a dish, the hair on the back of my neck often raises when I am tempted to over-torque a preparation by bending it to my will.

I remember cooking for my mom for the first time since going into Chicago and working at some fancy restaurants and reading some current magazines. Nouvelle cuisine was all the rage and fish with fruit sauce was everywhere. After reading a popular food magazine, I returned home to impress my mother with a modern approach. I picked a couple of superb tomatoes from her garden—they couldn't have been riper. I wanted the highest "brix" (a term I had just learned) possible. I split them and roasted them with honey, verbena, and Tahitian vanilla beans for a "nouveau" dessert that would be sure to impress my mentor. Mom's response could not have been more perfectly humbling: "What the hell did you do to that perfectly good tomato!?" Tail between my legs and ego bruised, thankfully, I returned to Chicago, never to make dessert out of another tomato.

Don't get me wrong. I believe in, support, and applaud the work of those who take food and cuisine to the very brink of culinary disaster in order to create celebrations of nature like no one has ever seen. I fully understand creative tension and how such tension has informed and propelled all art in ways that keep it living, breathing, ever changing, exhilarating. I just know that, tempting as it is to be seen as someone at the head of the wave, I feel most grounded in moving forward by glancing back. I feel compelled to work to bring us back to the simple whispers of our culture that once defined us a nation of good food, good neighbors, and sensible abundance. Perhaps I can help by providing a counterweight to help balance the work of those who forge forward into new brilliant technological realms with the honesty of what we have already developed and nearly lost.

So here I travel about the country and the globe in search of the projects and works that will spiritually and intellectually define me. I find myself trying to be more like Mom, while feeling drawn to the new and unusual. I do this in search of the way to bring my past and present together. Like my mom, I have a large vegetable garden, and like my mom, I try to cook simple meals for my family as often as my schedule will permit. She knew only Southern country cooking—the cooking of her childhood. I know this, too, but have been bombarded by the influence of a variety of cultures and sophisticated cooking methods. I have cooked my way around the world without ever leaving my kitchen until recently. I have created a cuisine that generated numerous menus in which not a single item contained added animal fat, cream, butter, or processed flours and sugars. I've written books and articles and have been fortunate enough to be occasionally celebrated. I feel obligated to share this journey with my children, friends, and the many I cook for, yet something inside me keeps pulling at me to return "home."

I have spent a decade silently struggling to reconcile my culinary heritage, which is down-home American country, with my desire to cook healthfully and to take full advantage of extensive training and cutting-edge technology.

The life I have now is one I couldn't imagine when I was growing up on my grandpa's farm and in my mother's kitchen. Then, my universe was my family, my school, my friends, the farm, kitchen, and garden. Now, my universe embraces all the wonders of the world. I am blessed with a loving wife and five children, I have traveled the country and much of the globe, I have worked in some of the best kitchens in Chicago, New York City, and elsewhere, and I count some of the finest people in the food business among my dearest friends.

Through it all, I always come back to Mom and what her garden and her kitchen meant to me. I hope my work is useful. She always wanted me to be helpful when I grew up.

Bugnes de Lyon

Daniel Boulud and Dorie Greenspan

This is my mother's recipe for a well-known Lyonnaise dessert, *bugnes*, or fried dough. Hometown pride makes me wish I could claim that Lyon is the only place you can find *bugnes*, but they are also popular throughout France and in Switzerland, where they are called *merveilles*, or marvels. In the United States, they are beloved in New Orleans. At home, my mother flavored the egg-rich dough with grated orange zest and formed the pastries into fanciful knot shapes before frying them. If you'd like, you can just roll out the dough and cut it into circles, squares, strips, or diamonds, small or large—they all look good and taste great. Whatever the shape, you should serve these freshly made, hot and showered with confectioners' sugar.

1½ teaspoons unsalted butter, at room
    temperature

1 teaspoon sugar

Pinch of salt

1 large egg

Grated zest of ½ navel orange

Rounded ¼ teaspoon baking powder

1 cup plus 2 tablespoons all-purpose flour

3 tablespoons whole milk

Peanut oil for deep-frying

Confectioners' sugar for dusting

1. Using a wooden spoon (as my mother would) or working in a mixer fitted with the paddle attachment, beat the butter, sugar, and salt together until creamy. Add the egg and beat well, then beat in the orange zest. Stir the baking powder into the flour and then stirl the flour into the bowl alternately with the milk, incorporating the flour in three additions and the milk in two. Turn the dough out onto a counter—or just reach into the bowl—and knead the dough lightly to form it into a ball. Cover the dough with plastic wrap and chill it in the refrigerator for at least 1 hour or, preferably, overnight.

2. Dust a baking sheet with flour and keep it close at hand. To shape the *bugnes* as my mother does, roll the dough out on a lightly floured work surface into a rectangle that's ¼ to ⅛ inch thick—these shouldn't be too thin. Cut the dough into 2-inch-wide strips and, using a sharp knife or a pastry cutter, cut each strip on

the diagonal at 2-inch intervals—you'll have created diamonds. Now, cut a 1½-inch-long slit down the center of each piece of dough—the slit should run down the length of the diamond. Take the top or bottom corner of the dough and lift it up and into the slit, then pull it out the other side—you'll have created a twisted handkerchief-like knot. Place the *bugnes* on the floured baking sheet, cover them with plastic wrap, and refrigerate for 1 hour.

3. Pour at least 4 inches of oil into a deep pot and heat it to 350°F, as measured on a deep-fat thermometer. Line a baking sheet with a double thickness of paper towels and keep the baking sheet and a slotted spoon close at hand.

4. Drop 5 or 6 *bugnes* into the oil—you don't want to crowd the pot—and fry for about 2 minutes, or until the underside of each *bugne* is golden. Turn the *bugnes* over and fry for another 2 minutes or so, just until the second side is also golden. Lift the *bugnes* out of the oil with a slotted spoon and place them on the towel-lined baking sheet to drain. Repeat with the remaining *bugnes*.

To serve: Sprinkle the pastries generously with confectioners' sugar and serve them while they're still warm.

To drink: A *verveine* infusion or an espresso with Cointreau on the side

Makes 20 to 25 bugnes.

Sweet Finale

Joyce White

By my last year of high school Aunt Mary's savings were dwindling, and since she had made her living from a back-porch beauty shop, she was making do with a very small pension check. Uncle John had long retired as a musician, and even though he was secretive and stingy, I think his finances were tight, too.

I don't know exactly when she decided to supplement her income with day work, and I don't know exactly whom she worked for, for she only referred to her employer, rather obliquely, as "Miss Lady." And then airily, "Just a day or two every week dusting and keepin' company."

I remember my last visit with her before I left home for college in the early 1960s. Her house was about a half-mile from the sea in a bustling African American neighborhood in Gulfport-Biloxi, Mississippi. In midafternoon, lonely without her presence, I ventured to the front porch, eagerly awaiting her arrival home for work.

Soon the city bus rolled to a stop just down the street from her house, and I watched her descend, dressed in a simple black dress and wearing a little black hat with a veil, set at a rakish angle. She walked, gingerly at first, and then picked up her gait and fell into the same hip-hop bouncy steps that I now see in my son, Roy, and my brother, Joe, which must be a genetic patterning.

She pushed open the front gate, looked up at me, burst out into laughter, and said, "Look what the cats have dragged to my front porch."

Levity graced my thoughts. In less than an hour we were scurrying about fixing supper, getting ready to tackle the crossword puzzle contest in the New Orleans *Times-Picayune*, her late afternoon ritual. Out in the dining room a bowl of salted or candied pecans or homemade candy for nibbling sat on the old mahogany table.

I was in my late teens then, and although the women in my family cooked virtually every day, by that time I knew that each one had a special touch with certain dishes. Aunt Mary was an expert candy maker and she wasn't shy about acknowledging her expertise. On the other hand, my oldest sister,

Helen, who was the head cook at a local cafe in rural Choctaw County in Alabama, where we lived, and later the personal cook for a rich family, made ethereal cakes, rich and luscious ice cream, and artisan chocolate desserts, but was modest to no end. Mama's pies and cobblers were nonpareil; Aunt Agnes (my maternal great-aunt) made scrumptious cookies, especially pale vanilla wafers scented with grated lemon peel, and crispy, crunchy benne or sesame wafers. Some historians say that African slaves arrived in the Carolinas carrying sesame seeds, which they believed brought good luck!

But it was Aunt Mary who wielded the most influence over both my academic and culinary pursuits, for although she was a skilled cook and a fanciful candy maker, her interests were wide-ranging and diverse.

Aunt Mary lived on the Gulf Coast in Mississippi, some 150 miles southwest of our home in rural Alabama, which was 75 or so miles north of Mobile. Sometime between 1915 and 1920, she and her six siblings, along with my grandfather and grandmother, fled the raging Tombigbee River, where they toiled and lived on water's edge in Clarke County, Alabama. The flooding river wiped out King Cotton, bringing starvation in its wake to tenant farmers and sharecroppers.

Daddy relocated to Mobile, became a dockworker, and later migrated to Choctaw County, where he met and married Mama. Two other brothers settled in on the Gulf Coast at

Pascagoula, one sister moved to the Mississippi Delta, and two other sisters went up north to Philadelphia, Pennsylvania, never to reunite again as a family.

My beautiful Aunt Mary kept on the move. After living on the Gulf Coast for several years, she went out west to Los Angeles, took a course in cosmetology, and dabbled at acting. She eventually returned to Gulfport-Biloxi in the early 1940s, and met and married a jazz trumpet player, John Collins, who was from a rather prominent family of musicians in New Orleans. By then she was in early midlife, a hairdresser by trade, an independent woman who operated her business from a little room on her back porch.

In 1949, shortly after high school, my oldest brother, John, left home and went to live with Aunt Mary, searching for a better life. And when I reached my teen years I visited her often, attracted by family lore. But as I reflect, it was actually Mama who encouraged my visits, for although she used to say quite disparagingly that "Mary died and went to heaven when she married that Collins music man," there was begrudging admiration. Aunt Mary was generous and gregarious, worldly, and witty, a "star" to her provincial relatives.

I thought her life was touched by magic. Throughout her house there were framed copies of her cosmetology diploma, and scores of photographs of her only child, daughter Victoria, and of Victoria's only child, Mary Ethel, who lived in faraway

Los Angeles. Aunt Mary's husband, a thin, fair-skinned, brooding, self-described "Creole," had a fine reputation in New Orleans jazz circles. He was always picking up his horn and blowing a few bars, the music hot and strange to my country ears, his raspy, hoarse voice startling.

To me, Aunt Mary's house was as grand as the rich white landowners' mansions. This was the late 1950s, and through the eyes of an adolescent I saw a lumpy chesterfield sofa in nape-worn velvet, elegantly revealing its age and pedigree. Two overstuffed side chairs covered with floral cretonne flanked the sofa, and there was a glass-topped rectangle walnut coffee table displaying another compendium of photographs. Several cluttered end tables held porcelain lamps with tattered fringed shades, and in one corner stood an old boxlike Victrola, which often flooded the room with cool jazz and country blues as soon as we finished working the crossword puzzle. I fell helplessly under her spell.

I can still see her the day she made gumbo for her club members at Mercy Seat Baptist Church. I had never eaten this legendary seafood dish before, and since my beloved aunt loved showing off, she began spouting off about the intricacies of gumbo. She said the dish came out of the slave kitchens of New Orleans, first as a Lenten dish for the masters, using only greens, a variation of the one-pot dishes of Africa.

For most of the day before the club meeting she scurried

about in the kitchen chopping the celery and onions and pepper, cleaning shellfish, stirring the roux or the gravy base, tasting the broth for flavor. From time to time she would throw back her head, set her arms akimbo, and lecture about the subtleties of this famous dish, with that ever-present Lucky Strike stuck in the corner of her mouth. (She lived to be eighty-eight.)

"Most folks think that you just throw a whole bunch of stuff in a pot and you got a gumbo," said my aunt, with a theatrical air, Hollywood style. "A gumbo is like a good stage production, you got to make it act by act. In layers. If you don't do that you end up with a real mess."

And with that said, she threw back her head laughing, and continued producing her show, me her audience, captivated by her stellar performance.

The next day shortly before 2 P.M. a half-dozen late-middle-aged church sisters filed up the walkway, onto the front porch, and knocked lightly on the door before entering.

"Hi, child," "Hi, girl," "Hi, hon," the ladies said to me almost in unison as I rushed to greet them, and then brushed past me and into the living room.

One of the women looked in my direction, said offhandedly over her shoulder, "Growin' up cute," and then called to the kitchen, "How you doin', Mary?"

In minutes my beloved aunt bounded out of the kitchen, placed a big steaming bowl of gumbo on a mat in the center of her old dining table, stepped back, and bowed ever so slightly.

"Gumbo!" a woman named Mrs. Cora shouted, her voice inflected with genuine surprise. "Mary, how could you!"

But it is the pecans that sear my memories of my dear aunt, who worked culinary magic with the nuggets she gathered from six heavy-bearing trees in her backyard. The pecans were big and plump, shells smooth, meat deeply ridged and flavorful, like sweet buttermilk. Whenever I visited we cracked and ate the pecans out of hand or roasted with spices and a sprinkling of salt. Sometimes she would boil up a burnt sugar glaze and drizzle it over the nuts for quick candied pecans, though she was a self-proclaimed expert at that famed Southern candy, pralines.

"Don't ever attempt to make pralines on a hot, muggy day," I heard her say many, many times. "You end up with a sticky mess."

She also stirred pecans into pies, coconut fudge, caramels, and brownies; folded them into quick breads; used them with frosting and icing on cakes. And she made delicious sand tart cookies, which in the South are also known as pecan sables, after the French word for sand. The sand tarts have a delectable crumbly, or "gritty," texture. And since she was generous to a fault, she often passed off a nicely wrapped box of candies and sweets to friends and neighbors, the receiver being whomever she was on speaking terms with at the moment.

Aunt Mary wasn't lean and linear like Daddy, or light brown with shoulder-length hair like Mama, but she was pretty in her own way. She was of medium stature, bosomy, and had an inquisitive, cocoa brown face set with oval eyes that were often squinted either with cigarette smoke, merriment, or wonder. She was fleet of feet, which left her in constant motion, as if she would never, ever have the time to do all the things she wanted to do, or was capable of doing.

"Sassy," says my brother John, summing up our aunt whenever our conversations flow back to the past and wash up the spirit of our ancestors. "Aunt Mary always talked back. In more than one way."

The last time I saw my dear aunt she sized me up with squinted eyes through a halo of cigarette smoke, before tossing out a witty repartee. It was the summer of 1969, and I remember the precise day because I was wearing a handkerchief-sized miniskirt, a little pink floral number, and was sporting a bushy Afro hairdo that made me look as thin as Twiggy. I had finished college and was now living in the Big Apple, New York City.

"There is no modesty there," my aunt greeted me, laughing, grabbing my hands and eyeing me with outstretched arms.

I flinched, wondering if she was just wittily playing on Gertrude Stein's words about Oakland, California, or if my appearance was really that startling. I felt during those days that my family was always "on" me—about my nappy hair and too-short clothes, about traveling all over to strange foreign countries, and most of all, about being insanely in love with a mad brother who was going to overthrow the government—tomorrow. And fighting back, I often threw verbal salvos, too.

She gauged my reaction and quickly added: "But other than that you look absolutely fabulous."

I laughed, and let her finely executed reproach go.

When I returned to the Gulf Coast in the summer of 1981 on my way back to New York from a year's stay in California, Aunt Mary was nearing the end of her life. My brother John still lives only a short distance from her old house, and despite his urging, I decided against seeing her during her last days, a decision I now regret. But I have sweet final memories, such as this:

She is hunched over the New Orleans *Times-Picayune*, which is spread out on her old dining-room table. Two small cut-glass bowls sit nearby, one piled with spicy salted pecans, the other holding the candied variation. Her eyes are squinted, and she is alternately drawing on a cigarette and sipping that strong chicory-laced coffee.

Uncle John is in his room, morose and grouchy, listening to

jazz, not the least concerned with our presence. It is spring break, early 1960s. The scene is forlorn and seductive: Gulf sea glistening in the distance, dull drone of traffic wheezing by, my beloved aunt in deep thought, yours truly riffling an old Winston dictionary at her command, daily crossword puzzle our pursuit, her unending passion. I am her aide-de-camp.

Aunt Mary pushes a little bowl of the aromatic candied pecans at me and I try not to stuff myself. Stammering and talking to herself, she tells me about *faux amis* and double entendres. She throws out a word to me and I look it up in her old battered dictionary. I offer a suggestion and she gives me an appreciative look. When the word doesn't fit she chides me for my error.

"Come on, sweetheart," she says, feigning exasperation, Lucky Strike cigarette at a jaunty angle. "You can do better than that. Find me a word that means . . ."

I wonder to myself how in the world could a woman who has been denied a formal education by a cruel apartheid school system know so much, but I am too much in awe to ask.

Finally she is satisfied with her answers. I slip on my blue car coat and she playfully pushes me toward the door. I rush to the post office, hoping to beat out the other contestants with an early postmark.

We never win. The next day we begin our pursuit again, nibbling on crunchy, barely sweet candied pecans, undaunted.

In the End Is the Beginning

James Villas

Although the June sun overhead is already hot enough to make the early morning air feel heavy, Mother sports a white long-sleeve shirt, a pair of loose khaki pants, and a spiffy straw hat as we leave the car and make our way deep into the remote, vast strawberry field on the north fork of eastern Long Island.

"Don't say I didn't warn you about wearing that skimpy golf shirt and those shorts," she nags, linking the handle of her large bucket over one arm while trying to position a small stool between two rows of bushes laden with fat, ripe strawberries. "Haven't you learned after all these years that chiggers will eat you alive?"

She leans down, plucks three luscious berries from the middle of one plant, and studies them carefully in the palm of her hand. "Lord, have you ever seen such beautiful berries? Pretty as our Southern ones, I do believe. And it looks like these bushes haven't even been touched. A dollar a quart. Can you imagine? Almost like the old days."

By the time I've begun picking not far away, Mother has already cleaned berries off the tops and centers of at least three plants and is maneuvering to sit on her stool in order to negotiate the full clusters down below.

"Ugh," she moans in exasperation, hesitant to lower her ample girth squarely on the stool till she's absolutely sure that it's firmly in place on the ground. "Honey, you better give me a hand over here," she directs. "I just can't pick the way I used to with these old joints. Makes me mad as a hornet."

Once she's settled, I watch momentarily as she resumes her labor with almost childlike enthusiasm, her short, chubby fingers rummaging about the clusters as she gathers the choicest berries and drops them carefully into the bucket. Already beads of perspiration have begun to drip from her silver hairline down her wrinkled face, and as she manipulates the fragile berries and globules of scarlet juice gradually stain the glabrous skin on the back of her hand, I notice how the surface blue veins and patches of brown spots only reinforce the fact that she's well into her eighth decade of life.

"Make sure you also pick the stems, so the berries don't bleed," she blurts as I return to my area. "And, for heaven's sake, son, do watch out for chiggers!"

Watch out for chiggers. . . . Watch out for chiggers. . . . The words ring in my memory, transporting me, for a moment, back some fifty-five or so years to a large strawberry field in Union County, North Carolina, about twenty miles from our home in Charlotte. It was another early warm June morning, and there, along with me, my youngest sister, Mother and Daddy, were my grandparents, Maw Maw and Paw Paw. At the edge of the field, an old farmer at his wooden stand passed out cardboard quart boxes, collected fifty cents a box, and told us that there were plenty of Cokes on ice in his red and white cooler.

"Remember, y'all: the bushes are always fuller at the far end of the rows," Daddy reminded everybody as we followed him deep into the field.

From time to time, my sister and I would pop the largest, reddest, warm sweet berries into our mouths, only to hear Paw Paw warn, "You young'ins better watch out. Didn't I tell you that if you eat too many strawberries, they'll grow bushes in your stomachs?"

"Lord have mercy," Maw Maw exclaimed out loud, getting up from her stool after about thirty minutes, checking her boxes, and peering over at Mother. "You know, Martha Pearl, if we keep picking at this rate, we're gonna have enough strawberries for preserves, shortcake, *and* a big churn of ice cream."

Squatted in front of a large plant, Mother, her slender body clothed from head to toe and her long, radiant chestnut hair pulled back from her smooth face into a tight bun, was just standing up when I rushed over to proudly display my half-filled box of berries and continue picking next to her.

"Son, I see a little white on some of those strawberries," she reprimanded mildly, running her beautiful, still youthful fingers carefully through the lot, tossing the imperfect ones on the ground and holding up a medium-sized bright red berry for me to observe. "Now look, if you're gonna help me put up preserves, you've gotta pick the right berries and stop eating every . . ." She suddenly noticed me scratching the inside of my thigh as we started picking together. "Unhuh. Chiggers!" she exclaimed sternly, reaching over to inspect my legs. "You wouldn't listen to me and your daddy when we told you about wearing shorts, and now . . . I'm telling you: you've got to watch out for chiggers!"

By ten o'clock, the Long Island sun is blazing. Our buckets overflowing with exquisite berries, Mother and I return to the rough country road to pay the farmer for our bounty, then drive to my home on the south fork so she can begin immediately to make the preserves that will last us through the year and help fill all her holiday gift packages. For years at home in North Carolina, Mother was never at a loss for relatives to participate in this annual summer ritual. But time passes, people disappear for one reason or another, and today there's only Mother and me left to carry on a tradition that is as sacred to her as making fruitcakes for Christmas. Of course every June when she comes to visit me on Long Island, she complains about her stiff knees and weak hands and threatens not to go strawberry picking. Then, after she rages about the poor quality and outrageous prices of market berries, prompting me to suggest that we just ride over and check the north fork field, she inevitably forgets her ailments and off we go.

"I need a drink," she announces in the kitchen, reaching for the Bloody Mary mix while I begin rinsing some ten quarts of strawberries and placing them on paper towels spread out over every inch of counter space. "Now, sort them carefully, honey, and make sure the ones for preserves are firm and the same size," she instructs as if I hadn't been through the process a hundred times over the years. She then opens a new package of pectin, measures cups of sugar, and takes a big slug of her restorative libation.

Cooking strawberries for preserves is a very serious and private affair for Mother, and nobody, not even my neighbor Craig Claiborne when he was alive, would ever risk distracting her. Once the hulled berries are in a big kettle and the first measurement of sugar is added, I step away as she brings the mixture very slowly to a boil and begins stirring attentively with a large wooden spoon. More sugar, a little lemon juice, a slight heat adjustment, then further careful stirring as she quietly watches the berries gradually yield their juices, blend with the melted sugar, and almost magically turn a deep, glistening red. Her concentration is intense.

"Quick, help me move this pot off the heat," she suddenly directs, lifting one side of the large vessel up before I can grab the other side.

"I thought you said you have no strength left in your hands," I jest.

"Hush. I don't have time to think about that now," she huffs, stirring pectin into the mixture. "Have you got those bowls ready?"

Together we slowly pour the hot berries into two large mixing bowls, after which Mother begins the tedious but important task of skimming foam off the tops so that the preserves will not be cloudy.

"Here," she says, handing me the spoon, "stir them steadily till they cool slightly and begin to thicken. I'm dead." She wipes her hands on her apron and reaches for her drink.

Quite often, the cooled strawberries must stand overnight so that they will jell and plump enough to remain in suspension when preserved. After we've had lunch and taken well-deserved naps, however, Mother determines by early evening that the texture and consistency of the berries are already ideal, rousing her to begin sterilizing half-pint canning jars and lids in a steaming water bath while I melt paraffin in a saucepan. At one point, she drops a lid on the floor and asks me to pick it up, complaining about how she can't bend down that far.

"Sometime I'd like to drop a hundred-dollar bill on the ground and watch you scramble for *that!*" I jeer.

"Smart aleck," she mumbles, popping me on the rear.

As I ladle luxurious preserves into the jars, Mother, with her experienced and expert touch, pours hot paraffin over the tops, slowly tilts each jar back and forth till the waxy substance begins to set and seal every edge, and caps each with a lid and ring band as a precaution against any improbable but always possible seepage. We then take each jar and apply a label that reads "From Martha's Kitchen."

"Pretty, aren't they?" Mother comments quietly, standing back with her tired hands on her hips and surveying the twenty-odd jars lined up across the counter. "But, Lord, that's a lot of work and . . . Well, honey, I really do think my strawberry-picking days are over."

Playfully I put my arm around her broad waist, tell her not to be so ridiculous, and suggest that she go change clothes so I can take her for a good dinner. Outside, the warm setting summer sun now filters gently through the towering oak trees, and as I gaze wistfully at this season's fresh, brilliantly red preserves that will bring such happiness to so many, I'm once again seized by all sorts of confused childhood, adolescent, and even recent nostalgia pertaining to the lady known to family as Martha Pearl, to friends simply as Martha, and to me as Mother, Missy, Big Mama, and, when she gets particularly overbearing, Brunhilde.

MOTHER'S STRAWBERRY PRESERVES

1 quart fresh, ripe, firm strawberries, stemmed
  and washed
4 cups granulated sugar
2 teaspoons fresh lemon juice
2 tablespoons pectin (Certo)

If the strawberries are very large, cut them in half. In a large saucepan, combine the strawberries and 2 cups of the sugar. Bring slowly to a boil and cook rapidly 5 minutes, stirring all the while. Add the remaining sugar, return to a boil, and cook 10 minutes longer, stirring in the lemon juice about 2 minutes before removing pan from heat. Add the pectin and stir well.

Pour the mixture into a large mixing bowl. Skim off as much foam as possible, cover with plastic wrap, and let stand till the berries are fully plump (at least 6 hours and possibly overnight), stirring occasionally.

Spoon the strawberries into hot, sterilized jars and seal with hot paraffin. When the paraffin is fully cooled, screw lids onto the jars. Store the preserves in a cool area and let age at least 2 months.

I can't remember everything exactly, but I know the war was still raging overseas and that, due to strict rationing, Mother was forced to use not only white margarine instead of butter, but also minimum sugar for the jelly treats I'd help her make. It's my first memory of cooking with her, a happy time when she'd show me how to roll small balls of dough between the palms of my hands, make indentions in the balls with a floured finger, then fill the holes with smidgeons of her home-made preserves. My next responsibility was to watch the cookies carefully as they baked. If I started fooling around while Mother was busy with other cooking and allowed them to overbrown, the tongue-lashing would be severe—followed, of course, by a consoling hug and explanation of why I had to learn to pay more attention to serious matters like baking cookies and making biscuits and . . .

"Son, if I've told you once, I've told you a hundred times not to handle the dough so much," she fumes when we're making buttermilk biscuits some years later. As usual, she has used only soft Southern Red Band flour and Crisco shortening, measured none of the ingredients, and is watching like a hawk every move I make. Disregarding the timer as she peeps through the glass on the oven door, she commands, "Take 'em out, they're done." To my eye, the biscuits don't appear nearly brown enough, and I say so. "I'm telling you to take 'em out *this second* or they'll be hard as rocks," she insists as I continue to argue. "Lord, how stubborn can you be?" Out they come, and sure enough, despite the unmeasured ingredients, and reduced cooking time, and my wounded pride, the biscuits are as puffy and even and golden and perfect as every batch she's ever baked to accompany our beloved short ribs of beef. . . .

"You've been playing around again, and you've absolutely ruined these ribs," she barks after a first bite of short ribs I've modified by adding green olives and a few fresh herbs. "You know, Buster, you still haven't gotten it through your thick head that the secret of great Southern food is its natural simplicity. Southern short ribs of beef are *not* French pot-au-feu (pronounced "potty foo").

French pot-au-feu. Just the name evokes still another random, distant image of Mother sitting on the edge of her and Daddy's bed in her frilly nightgown and dropping quarters into small paper cylinders. Times are still lean after the war. Daddy has a job selling trucks after having worked for the government supervising the local rationing of gasoline, but nothing will do but for Mother to save enough money so that we can splurge one night at a fancy French restaurant during a planned trip to New York City to visit relatives. That extra money might well go toward a down payment for a washing machine or be spent on a new dress. She knows, however, that Daddy is eager to take her, my sister, and me to a deluxe restaurant he's heard about called Le Chambord, and as she sees it, what does another small personal sacrifice matter if she can help to make her family happy? So she collects her quarters and dollar bills month after month, she even finds a way to buy me a new blue suit for the anticipated occasion, and at the restaurant she and Daddy order a glorious pot-au-feu that she will insist for years to come is the greatest dish she's ever tasted.

No doubt food and cooking have always been the major catalyst in my long, complex, and often labored relationship with my mother. But to explain the most important force in my life merely in terms of gustatory affinities not only misrepresents this most sacred of unions, but reduces the close bond we've established over the past six decades to an almost casual substantiality. Thousands of sons have acknowledged either the beneficial or the malevolent influences of their mothers, usually from the perspective of an adult distanced by geography or marriage or both. As a single gay man, by contrast, I have always maintained the proverbial childhood link with my mother that psychiatrists love to analyze in such depth, an alliance that neither time nor space nor different lifestyles have ever altered in the least. Others come to refer to their mothers as a friend, a confidante, or a pal. My mother is none of these to me. She is simply my mother, the same mother who nursed and corrected and spanked me when I was a child, the one who taught me how to cook at her knee, and the irrepressible, feisty remarkable lady who can do no wrong. She's on a pedestal—and this, as I see it, is the way it should be.

Southerners tend to be family-oriented in the extreme. I never was and still have little in common with relatives other than my mother. I loved and respected my father in the ancient Greek tradition that is in my veins, and his influence on my social and intellectual development was profound—especially in the area of dining sophistication. But even his impact on my life was modest compared with that of Mother's. She was the family bulwark while I was growing up, the one who saw to it that I was never in need of clothing or money or attention, the one who encouraged me to take piano lessons even though she had no interest at all in classical music, the one who supervised my schooling and spent grueling hours helping me with homework, and of course, the one who instilled in me a love of cooking. No doubt Mother perceived instinctively at an early date that I was cut from a different cloth than that of my classmates—a loner determined to map out and follow his own direction. And when the time came for me to seek new horizons while my friends remained safely in the nest, it was Mother who never once questioned my intentions and lent full material and emotional support. She understood me.

Those who have read the three books that Mother and I have coauthored on her Southern cooking were exposed not only to her amazing culinary abilities, but also to multiple facets of our unique partnership in and out of the kitchen. They grow to know a gracious but stern lady who tolerates no nonsense when it comes to her vast legacy of Southern dishes, just as they became acquainted with a highly opinionated, often difficult, but respectful son. They followed us through peach orchards, oyster beds, blackberry patches, and remote mountain hamlets in search of luscious country hams. They learned how to cut up and fry chicken properly, make congealed salads and pimento cheese, and even produce Carolina pork barbeque. And they were privy to our heated debates over the most minute cooking problems, our constant fussing with one another, and the conflicts that erupt when two strong-minded individuals assert their sense of authority. All the arguments, cajoling, and hilarity were, of course, legitimate, and I think we did manage to convey the true spirit of Southern cooking. However, like most cookbooks, which by their very nature must project a superficial idealism that appeals to a mass middle-class audience, these hardly delved into the more intimate aspects of Mother's and my personalities or attempted to explain how we've managed to function so well together for so many years.

And contrary to certain impressions one might get from the books, our lives actually couldn't be more antithetical, a fact known only to our closest friends and one that has engendered more than a little frustration and, at times, anguish for us both. Mother is a very outgoing, social lady who gets along with anybody; I'm basically a solitary. Having had little education, she shares none of my literary or musical passions, the highlight of her weekday being a series of afternoon TV soap operas, which subject her apartment and my house to hours of romantic mush that drives me up the wall. A devoted fan of *Reader's Digest* and heartthrob novels, Mother can't imagine what I find engrossing about the London *Spectator*, *Opera News*, *The New Yorker*, and Kazuo Ishiguro, and she calls me a snob. When not discussing food or travel, her idea of engaging conversation revolves mostly around family and others' children, subjects I find repellant. She forever challenges my deep-rooted cynicism with her eternal optimism, and while I'm a self-centered, neurotic misanthrope, her compassion for others is as selfless as it is genuine. I envy her sunny disposition and wish I could imitate it.

For whatever reasons, much of our respective lives remains shrouded in or camouflaged by enigma and paradox. Why around Mother, for instance, my Southern accent suddenly deepens and my overall vocabulary and mien become almost sloven I can't explain. Generally, I curse like a drunken sailor, but in front of my mother, I can't bring myself to utter so much as an innocuous "damn"—much less a more characteristic "goddamn." While I do consult her on virtually every food topic I write about, a literary profile or a piece of fiction is work that I keep confidential. Nothing is more important to Mother than her religious beliefs and involvement in the church, but since I gave up on God decades ago, her fervor remains a very private and mysterious affair. As for my homosexuality, the subject has never once been broached and probably never will be. First, I respect fully that Southern ladies of my mother's generation have never been comfortable confronting openly such delicate matters. Second, even when I was young and active, I never felt the need to reveal and deliberate my sexuality with my parents, and to do so today with Mother would be an exercise that even she would find ludicrous and embarrassing. No doubt her wise motherly instincts informed her of my libidinous proclivities long before I myself came to terms with my sexual makeup, and while I know she wouldn't hesitate a moment to discuss this facet of my life if I so chose,

I also know that our Southern breeding has always precluded sex on any level as an appropriate topic of conversation. And that's the way it should be.

I am one who fiercely believes that it's a son's or daughter's moral duty to repay parents who made tough and repeated sacrifices to assure a child's well-being. In most areas and with most people, I hardly consider myself very charitable, but when it comes to my mother, I profess that much of my adult life has been spent trying to show my appreciation and bring the same happiness to her that she's given to me and so many others. Not that I pretend to be noble, but I don't forget the deprivation of the war years, or the way she was forced for so long to care for not one but two aged grandmothers, or the utter hell she endured when my sister was stricken with a near-fatal brain aneurysm that rendered her an invalid and destroyed most of her personality. I remember the homemade cookies and toilet paper and extra money that Mother mailed three thousand miles away every month while I was a student in France. It made me proud that for more than twenty years she never once failed to send an enormous carton of baked Christmas goodies to the staff at *Town & Country*. And how could a son not be beholden to a mother who, on her own lone initiative and with typical authority, dealt with the deaths of two of my beloved dogs by combing the back roads of North Carolina till she found suitable replacements? No, indeed, the explanations of my filial devotion and love extend far beyond the narrow confines of a kitchen, and if it's no more in my neurasthenic nature to constantly hug and kiss and make a fuss over her the way others do so obligingly with a parent, I never doubt for a moment that she senses the emotions. And, I'm convinced, that's the way it should be.

In addition to giving Mother material goods as she did for me when I was young and needy, I also began years ago involving her in my professional food world—especially after my father died—in hopes that this would add new dimension to and perhaps prolong her very active and energetic life. Little did I know at the time how the casual collaboration would evolve, but the truth is that it not only produced three successful cookbooks, but turned Mother into an octogenarian celebrity, the darling of chefs and the media alike. Craig Claiborne and Pierre Franey used to beg her for recipes, Paul Bocuse adores her, Paula Wolfert calls her for cooking advice, and when she was invited to conduct classes at the prestigious Cipriani Cooking School in Venice, none other than Julia Child (there also to teach) engaged her in intense discussion on the correct way to make Southern fried chicken and buttermilk biscuits. She's demonstrated dishes on *Good Morning America*, the Food Network, and other national broadcast outlets, and when we were both interviewed recently aboard the *QE2*, the throngs who lined up afterward at a book signing were there to meet not me but my crazy mother. Of course, she pretends indifference to all the attention and rebels when I accuse her mockingly of being a ham, but I know that deep down she relishes it all. As for myself, I beam with pride and satisfaction.

SOUTHERN BUTTERMILK BISCUITS

2 cups all-purpose flour

4 teaspoons baking powder

½ teaspoon baking soda

½ teaspoon salt

¼ cup Crisco shortening

1 cup buttermilk

Preheat oven to 450°F.

Sift together the flour, baking powder, baking soda, and salt into a large mixing bowl, add the shortening, and cut it with a pastry cutter or two knives till the mixture is well blended and mealy. Add the buttermilk and mix with a large spoon till the dough is soft, adding a little more buttermilk if necessary.

Turn the dough out onto a lightly floured surface, and, using a light touch, turn the edges of the dough toward the middle, pressing with your hands. (Do not overwork the dough.) Press the dough out to a ¼-inch thickness (do not roll with a rolling pin), cut straight down into even rounds with a biscuit cutter or small juice glass, and place the rounds ½ inch apart on a large baking sheet.

Gather up the scraps of dough and repeat the procedure. Bake the biscuits just till lightly browned on top, about 12 minutes.

Makes about 16 biscuits.

Perhaps the most amazing and revealing aspect of my long association with Mother is how I perceive her uncanny wisdom today to be as sharp as when she was ruling the roost at home some half a century ago. After years of challenging her cooking ideas and techniques and, as she says, "fooling around," I've come to the grudging realization that, dammit, with few exceptions, she's always right in the kitchen. Her instinctive ability to whip up perfect fresh mayonnaise and virtually any style sauce without even glancing at her sacred but impossibly jumbled black "receipt" book, to turn out home-made bread and pastry with the same ease as she does intricate needlepoint, to butcher anything from a chicken to a thirty-pound pig, and to transform the most rudimentary of ingredients into sumptuous feasts with no more than her time-tested old battered pots and pans—these are talents and practices and habits that defy interference and make a mockery of most novelties in today's fickle culinary world. "You'll learn some-day, son," Mother has ribbed more often than I care to remember when I've done something stupid, "but just like when you were a child, you'll have to learn the hard way." Indeed.

Equally intimidating has been the way my tastes in food,

after years of putatively sophisticated transformation, have devolved almost inscrutably to those of my mother's. No longer, for example, do I like any fish or steak gussied up with a sauce. I'd rather have it simply broiled or grilled with minimum seasoning—and preferably at a fine seafood emporium or steak house. Beans and peas taste utterly bland unless they're fully cooked with a small piece of pork fat; a great shrimp and corn chowder is eminently more satisfying than a rich lobster bisque; and having for years rejected with contempt all congealed salads and meat casseroles, I now prepare and serve them as proudly and regularly as Mother does. Because of her, I've learned how delectable a full summer meal of nothing but fresh vegetables can be. She's taught me not only the virtues of using only soft winter flour for baked goods, only white cornmeal, and only Crisco shortening, but also convinced me that Greek feta cheese is far superior to Bulgarian, that no onion on earth can equal genuine Vidalias, that kosher and sea salts are overrated, and that the biggest rip-offs in gastronomic history are overpriced extra-virgin olive oils and balsamic vinegars. Mother has always loathed ketchup, and just in the past year, I've even noticed that I'm no longer squeezing it on my hamburgers. Don't ask me to explain.

While I've never subjected Mother intentionally to my emotional problems, she's quick to pick up on any mood changes, any hysterics, and any bouts with frustration and despair. Something so trivial as a glitch in our travel plans, a screwed-up restaurant reservation, or a punctuation change in a manuscript can so threaten my damnable perfectionism that I'm driven to distraction. And if I so much as casually allude to the problem, she still has that unique ability to grasp the issue immediately, empathize, and, if necessary, reprimand sternly.

"As I used to tell your daddy," I've heard her bark more than once when she sensed that my complaint was exaggerated or foolish, "it's absurd to get upset over something you can't do anything about. There're just too many other important things to worry about in this life to allow a bunch of nonsense to get you down. So shape up." Of course, it's shameful to realize that I'm still being addressed as a child, but curiously, after one of her facile but wise lectures, the distress does seem to disappear. As it should.

Where Mother and I do differ radically is in our individual lifestyles, a factor that creates some tension when we spend long periods of time together traveling or working on a cookbook. Alone in her apartment, she likes a noon lunch followed by her soaps, her thoughts begin dwelling on the Jack Daniel's bottle by late afternoon, and she prefers to dine no later than eight o'clock and retire early. I, by contrast, am accustomed at home to putting off lunch (especially when writing) till midafternoon, not starting cocktails till well after dark, eating around ten, and often not going to bed till two in the morning.

Somehow we reach a compromise when she visits or we're traveling, but only after considerable haggling and her reminding me repeatedly how ridiculously eccentric and abnormal my way of life has become. Also, I must have an afternoon nap no matter where, which irritates her almost as much as her soaps drive me nuts. I've always suspected that this is what marriage must be like, and when I say so, she simply glares suspiciously, then rolls her eyes the way she does when I ask a dumb question about cooking.

Since we both religiously eat three well-balanced meals a day, much of our time together is spent either shopping for food and cooking or going to restaurants. Neither of us pays the least bit of attention to the possible dangers of excess weight, cholesterol, alcohol, and the like; and pity the poor soul who dares to bring up the subject of dieting around my mother.

"Listen," she once coldly informed a certain zealous health fanatic, "my mamma lived into her nineties and ate bacon and cornbread every day of her life. I'm in my eighties and over-weight, but I eat anything I want, I drink plenty of wine and hard liquor, I've never swallowed a single vitamin pill, and I'm still going strong. Jimmy never diets, either, and if he'd just stop smoking those stinking cigarettes, he'd probably live as long as I have."

It's true that for her age, Mother is remarkably fit and independent, so much so that despite my worry and futile protests, she thinks nothing of loading the trunk of her big Buick with sacks of Southern flour, pickling ingredients, a country ham, fresh butter beans and tomatoes, an ice cream churn, bottles of cut-rate Jack Daniel's, and Lord knows what else and driving seven hundred miles from Charlotte to East Hampton. Yet every time I notice the thinning silver hair and vaporous blue eyes, detect a momentary languor in her otherwise alert voice, or watch her bravely negotiate a set of stairs as the tyranny of time claims victory over her knees, I do wonder how many more berry-picking days are left.

When she complains occasionally about decrepitude, I simply tell her it's laziness or all in her head, and since this infuriates her, I go a step further and project that she'll outlive me—not an unlikely prospect given my reckless ways. The reality, of course, is that now I can't imagine a world without the mother who's always been there to teach, encourage, console, and accept what others can't tolerate. The author William Maxwell said it all when he spoke of the "shine" that disappeared from his life after his mother's death. That's no doubt a sobering insight, but at least for the time being, I know that as long as Big Mama is still around to roam farmers' markets, bake fruitcakes, put up pickles for friends, and remind me about chiggers, the universe remains a bright place where warm strawberry fields extend forever.

Credits and Permissions

"The Measure of My Powers" from *The Art of Eating 50th Anniversary Edition* by M. F. K. Fisher. Copyright © 1937 by M. F. K. Fisher. Reprinted with permission of John Wiley & Sons, Inc.

"Bread-and-Butter Pudding" from *Toast: The Story of a Boy's Hunger* by Nigel Slater. Copyright © 2003 by Nigel Slater. Used by permission of Gotham Books, an imprint of Penguin Group (USA) Inc.

"Maman's Cheese Soufflé" from *The Apprentice: My Life in the Kitchen* by Jacques Pepin. Copyright © 2003 by Jacques Pepin. Reprinted by permission of Houghton Mifflin Company. All rights reserved.

About the Contributors

Maya Angelou is a poet, writer, performer, teacher, and director. In addition to her best-selling autobiographies, beginning with *I Know Why the Caged Bird Sings*, she has also written five poetry collections, including *I Shall Not Be Moved* and *Shaker, Why Don't You Sing?*, as well as the celebrated poem "On the Pulse of Morning," which she read at the inauguration of President William Jefferson Clinton, and "A Brave and Startling Truth," written at the request of the United Nations and read at its fiftieth anniversary. She lives in Winston-Salem, North Carolina.

Jennifer Appel owns midtown Manhattan's Buttercup Bake Shop, featuring old-fashioned American desserts. Previously, she cofounded and operated New York City's Magnolia Bakery. She is the author of *The Buttercup Bake Shop Cookbook*, and coauthor of *The Magnolia Bakery Cookbook*. Her third cookbook is due out in the fall of 2006.

Daniel Boulud is the chef-owner of two New York City restaurants, Café Boulud and Daniel, one of only six restaurants to earn *The New York Times*'s highest rating. He is also the author of *Cooking with Daniel Boulud*.

Holly Clegg is the author of the best-selling *Trim & Terrific* cookbook series, including *The Holly Clegg Trim & Terrific Cookbook, Holly Clegg Trim & Terrific Home Entertaining the Easy Way*, and *Eating Well Through Cancer*. She appears regularly on *Fox & Friends* and the NBC *Weekend Today* show and writes for several national publications. For more information, visit her Web site: www.hollyclegg.com.

M.F.K. Fisher was the author of numerous books of essays and reminiscences, many of which have become American classics.

Rosemary Gong is an Asian American writer and lecturer who lives within walking distance of San Francisco's Chinatown. A recipe for *gok jai* cookies can be found in her book, *Good Luck Life—The Essential Guide to Chinese American Celebrations and Culture*. For more information, visit her Web site www.goodlucklife.com.

Dorie Greenspan has written five cookbooks, among them the prizewinning *Baking with Julia*, to accompany Julia Child's television series, and *Desserts by Pierre Herme*.

Cliff Lowe's mother taught him to cook when he was six years old, and he became a self-taught chef working in restaurants and for private functions while maintaining a full-time job. His writing has appeared in *Science Digest*, *The Old Farmer's Almanac*, *Hypnosis*, and more. Cliff is retired, living for the last fourteen years in Canada, and now writes about cooking and the history of food for www.inmamaskitchen.com.

Royal Mack is a wine writer and teacher living in Los Angeles. She credits her aunt with getting her into wine and out of show business.

As the native-born daughter of one of the founders of the Black Dog restaurant, *Tina Miller* was exposed to the Vineyard restaurant scene at a young age. Miller gained her expertise as a chef by training at La Varenne in France and famed restaurants in Los Angeles and Philadelphia. She was the chef-owner of two beloved Vineyard restaurants, the Roadhouse and Cafe Moxie, and is the author of *Vineyard Harvest*. She works as a private chef and lives with her husband and sons on the Vineyard.

Award-winning author *Kitty Morse* was born in Casablanca and is the author of nine cookbooks, five of them on the cuisine of Morocco and North Africa. She leads an annual tour to Morocco, focusing on the country's food and culture. Kitty divides her time between Southern California and Dar Zitoun, her father's home on Morocco's Atlantic coast. The historic *riyad* is the focus of her next book, tentatively titled *Tales from the Kasbah*. You can view her Web site at www.kittymorse.com.

Lela Nargi is a writer and freelance reporter who lives in Brooklyn, New York. Her essays have appeared in *Natural Bridge*, *Gastonomica*, *Descant*, *Hotel Amerika*, and *The Ravel Chronicles*. She is the author of *All U Can Eat* and *Knitting Lessons*.

Michel Nischan pioneered his full-flavored, healthy cuisine at Heartbeat in New York. He can be seen on David Rosengarten's *In Food Today* and Sara Moulton's *Cooking Live*. He contributes regularly to *O*, the Oprah Winfrey magazine, and appears regularly on public television, the Food Network, and CNBC's new talk show for diabetes, "D-Life."

Christina Orchid has owned and operated her landmark Orcas Island restaurant, Christina's, since its doors opened in 1980. She has been featured in numerous magazines, including *Bon*

Appétit and *Food & Wine*, and is the author of *Christina's Cookbook*. She lives in Westsound on Orcas Island in Washington State.

Jacques Pepin is the author of twenty-one cookbooks, including *Jacques Pepin Celebrates* and, with Julia Child, *Julia and Jacques Cooking at Home*. He has starred in thirteen PBS programs over the past twenty years.

Stella Mazur Preda's poetry has appeared in many literary journals and anthologies in Canada. She currently serves as president of the Tower Poetry Society (Hamilton, Ontario, Canada), Canada's oldest ongoing poetry organization. Her first book, *Butterfly Dreams*, was published in 2003, and at that time she started her own imprint, Serengeti Press, which features the works of new and established Canadian authors and poets.

Ruth Reichl is the editor in chief of *Gourmet* and the author of the best sellers *Tender at the Bone* and *Comfort Me with Apples*. Her latest book is *Garlic and Sapphires*. She has been the restaurant critic at *The New York Times* and the food editor and restaurant critic at the *Los Angeles Times*. Reichl lives in New York City with her husband and son.

Harriet Rochlin is a historian and novelist. She is the author of *Pioneer Jews: A New Life in the Far West*, *The Reformer's Apprentice: A Novel of Old San Francisco*, *The First Lady of Dos Cacahuates*, and *On Her Way Home*. Her Web site is www.rochlin-roots-west.com

Julie Sahni has written several award-winning books about the food of India, including the highly acclaimed *Classic Indian Cooking*. Her Indian Cooking School in New York City and biannual Culinary Splendors of India tours are renowned as among the nation's best.

Lisa Schroeder is the chef and owner of Mother's Bistro & Bar, Mama Mia Trattoria, and Balaboosta in Portland, Oregon. Mother's Bistro & Bar has been featured in many local and national publications, including *Food and Wine*, *Bon Appétit*, *Food Arts*, *Nation's Restaurant News*, *USA Today*, *The Oregonian*, and *Willamette Week*.

Diana Farrell Serbe is a writer and an actress. She is the creator and editor of the Web site www.inmamaskitchen.com.

Nigel Slater is the author of several classic cookbooks, including *Real Fast Food* and the award-winning *Appetite*. He has written a much-loved column for *The Observer* (London) for more than a decade, and lives in London.

A native of Pforzheim, Germany, where he began his culinary career at age four, *Walter Staib* is chef/proprietor of Philadelphia's historic City Tavern restaurant and president of Concepts By Staib, Ltd., a globally operating hospitality consulting company. Chef Staib is author of *City Tavern Cookbook* (1999) and *City Tavern Baking & Dessert Cookbook* (2003), and is currently writing *My Black Forest*, which will be published in fall 2006.

James Villas was the food and wine editor of *Town & Country* magazine for twenty-seven years. His work has also appeared in *Esquire*, *Food & Wine*, *Gourmet*, *Bon Appétit*, *The New York Times*, and many other publications. A recipient of the James Beard Award, Villas is the author of many cookbooks and books on food.

Martha Washington was the first First Lady of the United States, and was married to George Washington for forty years. When she died at age seventy on May 22, 1802, an Alexandria, Virginia, newspaper obituary reflected the sentiment of the entire nation in describing her as "the worthy partner of the worthiest of men."

Joyce White is the author of two memoir/cookbooks, *Soul Food: Recipes and Reflections from African-American Churches* and *Brown Sugar: Soul Food Desserts from Family and Friends*, both published by HarperCollins. She is also the former associate food editor of *Ladies' Home Journal* magazine, and was an award-winning reporter and editor at the *New York Daily News*. She currently writes a weekly column on food, wine, and travel, "Soul in the Kitchen," that appears in newspapers across the country, including the *Amsterdam News* in New York City and the *Star Tribune* in Minneapolis. Her work is also frequently syndicated by the Tribune Media Services.